TRY GIVING YOURSELF AWAY

A TONIC FOR THESE TROUBLED TIMES

ℨ TRY

GIVING YOURSELF

AWAY

By DAVID DUNN

THIRD EDITION

IN WHICH is set forth that happier way
of living which all of us so earnestly seek and
so few seem to find ... *This is a great pity*
since the secret lies within ourselves, and its
magic can be enjoyed every day *without price.*

Prentice-Hall, Inc.   *Englewood Cliffs, N.J.*

Try Giving Yourself Away
Third Edition
by David Dunn

LIBRARY OF CONGRESS CATALOG CARD NUMBER: 74–102032

PRINTED IN THE UNITED STATES OF AMERICA · *T*
0–13–932442–9

Prentice-Hall International, Inc., London
Prentice-Hall of Australia, Pty. Ltd., Sydney
Prentice-Hall of Canada, Ltd., Toronto
Prentice-Hall of India Private Ltd., New Delhi
Prentice-Hall of Japan, Inc., Tokyo

20 19 18 17 16 15 14 13 12 11

DEDICATION

TO EVERY MAN AND WOMAN

WHO IS SEEKING

GREATER HAPPINESS

IN THESE TROUBLED TIMES

A Book for the Times

Several years ago I wrote a brief article entitled ' Try Giving Yourself Away," which appeared anonymously in *Forbes Magazine* and was reprinted in an even more condensed version in *The Reader's Digest*. With the kind permission of these publishers, and at the request of many persons, I expanded that short article into a book, developing in considerable detail the Art of Giving-Away. In this book I tried to answer many questions that had been put to me by personal friends, and in letters from readers of the original article.

No sooner was the book in circulation than letters began pouring in on me from men and women and boys and girls from all walks of life. They wrote to tell me what the book meant to them, and how it was influencing their lives and making them happier persons.

As I gained experience in practicing my giving-myself-away hobby, and learned from the experience of others how it might be broadened and enriched, a second edition of the book was prepared, with four added chapters. More and more people wrote letters expressing their enthusiasm for my hobby. Their letters warmed my heart.

Since the publication of that second edition, much has been happening in the world. Some of it has been deeply distressing.

Things are taking place all around us to make daily living confusing and difficult. Some of the impulsive ways of giving ourselves to others which are described in this book might arouse suspicion. For example, it would be unwise today to give candy to strange children, for fear our motive might be misunderstood. But all of us can safely give a fleeting smile to any child we pass, for children have a right to grow up in a smiling world.

Or it would be inadvisable to attract unusual attention to ourselves in public places. But that need not keep us from quietly giving ourselves in thoughtful little ways to our neighbors and friends, and the people we contact on our job or while shopping.

✦ ✦ ✦

Never before in the history of the world has the *spirit* of giving ourselves away been as needed as it is today. There is so much that every one of us, no matter how great or how modest our talents, or how high or humble our stations in life, can quietly do in the routine of our lives, to cure at least *some* of the ills of our troubled times.

When the publishers suggested that I again update the book, I readily agreed. At first I thought to take out the impulsive actions related in some of the chapters, but I soon discovered that this spoiled the spirit and flow of the book. And I decided that the caution sounded above would suffice to put the reader on notice to use judgment in doing unusual things in public that might attract undue attention to the giver.

So, instead of leaving anything *out*, I have added a dozen *new* chapters appropriate to the times.

No reader needs to be reminded that the world is full of

strife and heartache. Men and women everywhere seek peace of mind and heart, and wish desperately that they as individuals could do *something* toward lifting the heavy blanket of gloom that oppresses mankind.

You and I *can* help. More than anything else, the world needs the healing influence of a great surge of simple *thoughtfulness* and *kindheartedness*. Such a surge is beyond the power of the world's rulers or statesmen. It must start with *us,* as individuals. Right in our home communities we average citizens can establish the spirit and set the pattern of a kindlier world.

Could there be a more opportune time for all of us to *try giving ourselves away?* Could anything else we might do as individuals contribute so much toward the peace of the world, or earn us so much personal happiness? I doubt it.

I invite you to join me in my hobby.

DAVID DUNN

Contents

TRY GIVING YOURSELF AWAY

I Make an Important Discovery

Like most people, I was brought up to look upon life as a process of *getting*. The idea of *giving myself away* came to me quite by accident, one night many years ago. I was making my monthly trip to Chicago on the Twentieth Century Limited, now but a nostalgic memory but then Queen of the Rails. Lying awake in my berth, I fell to wondering where the Chicago-bound and New York-bound Centuries passed each other in the night.

"That would make an interesting subject for one of the New York Central's advertisements," I said to myself—"Where the Centuries Pass." Whereupon I went to sleep.

I wrote a letter to the New York Central Lines presenting the idea, "with no strings attached." A few days later I received a courteous letter of acknowledgment and the information that the Centuries were scheduled to pass near the little town of Athol Springs, New York, nine miles west of Buffalo.

Some months later I received a second letter informing me that my "Where the Centuries Pass" idea would be used as the subject for the New York Central calendar for the coming year. The calendar showed a picturesque night picture of the oncoming steam locomotive of one Century and the lighted observation platform of the other, passing on a curve. It was a scene rich in color and the railroad romance of that day.

The following summer I traveled extensively. In almost every railroad station and hotel lobby I entered, both at home and in Europe, hung the Century calendar based on the idea I had given the railroad. It never failed to give me a glow of pleasure.

It was thus I made the important discovery that anything which makes one glow with pleasure is beyond money calculation, in this humdrum world where there is altogether too much grubbing and too little glowing.

I began to experiment with giving-away, and discovered it to be great fun. My life began to be full of exciting little adventures, and I found myself making many new friends.

I discovered, too, that successful giving-away has to be cultivated. There is a knack to it, just as there is to successful getting. Opportunities for reaping dividends of happiness are fleeting. You have to act quickly or they elude you. But that only adds zest to the enterprise!

One day I woke up to the fact that I was really a collector —a collector of Glows and After Glows. It is a fascinating hobby. Like collecting anything else, you are always looking for new experiences in giving-away to add to your collection. Unlike other forms of collecting, however, you need no safe or cabinet in which to keep your treasures; nor do you have to go out of your way to keep adding to your collection. You have only to look around, wherever you are, to discover some opportunity to give yourself away.

I recommend giving-away as an exciting and thoroughly satisfying hobby. In fact, if you will give it a good try, I'll practically guarantee you a happier life—starting right away!

Chapter 2

Capsule Adventures in Giving
—and Living

Your giving-away will, of course, have to be done in your own individual way, based on the things *you* have to give.

Fortunately each of us has a different assortment of gifts, so there could never be anything standardized about giving-away, even though every one of us were to take up the hobby. Some of us have spare time; others have surplus mental or physical energy; others have a special art, skill, or talent; still others have ideas, imagination, the ability to organize, the gift of leadership.

All of us can give appreciation, kindness, interest, loyalty, understanding, encouragement, tolerance—and a score of other little portions of ourselves. Each of us should "major" in the items in which we are "long," and fill in with the others.

Perhaps you will catch the idea faster if I explain how I practice my hobby.

Suppose I am passing a neighborhood store in which I notice a particularly attractive window display. I say to myself, "Someone put real thought into trimming that window, and he or she ought to know that at least one passerby appreciates it."

So I stop in, ask for the manager, and compliment him

on the display. I find it always pleases a merchant to know that his windows are noticed, even though I may not buy a penny's worth of the merchandise displayed in them. In one instance the clerk who trimmed the windows received a raise in pay as a result of my compliment.

✓ ✓ ✓

If I particularly enjoy a book, a magazine article, or a play, I write a note to the author, telling him or her of my enjoyment. Sometimes I receive an appreciative acknowledgment; more often I do not. It doesn't matter in the least; I am not collecting autographs; I am just keeping my giving-away machinery in good working order.

✓ ✓ ✓

One Saturday afternoon while working in my garden I thought of an idea which I believed a certain New York department store might find useful. That evening I wrote a letter to the store outlining the idea and presenting it, as is my custom, "with no strings attached." It was adopted with appreciation—and I had acquired a big department store as a friend.

✓ ✓ ✓

If an idea comes to me that I think could be used by a local priest, minister, doctor, lawyer, or merchant, I write him a note telling him about it, though he may be a stranger to me.

If in my reading I run across an article, a picture, a cartoon, or a poem that I think would interest some friend, or even a casual acquaintance, I clip it out and send it to the person. Sometimes I send clippings to total strangers.

*   *   *

One spring evening I stopped at a popcorn wagon in Battle Creek, Michigan. A couple of urchins watched hungrily as the melted butter was being poured on the freshly popped corn. Without seeming to notice the youngsters, I ordered two more bags, paid for them, handed each of the boys his bag, and strode away. This little adventure-in-giving made the world more exciting for four people that evening—for the popcorn vendor, too, enjoyed the episode.

*   *   *

The text of an advertisement in a trade magazine appealed to me as being a wonderfully fine piece of writing. I wrote a note to the company saying that, while I was not in the market for their service, I did want to compliment them on their advertisement. Some days later I received a letter from Philadelphia from the man who had written the advertisement. He said my note encouraged him no end and had given him fresh inspiration. I had acquired a new friend in Philadelphia. I have since had many fine letters from him.

*   *   *

One evening I was dining alone in a Boston hotel. The selections the orchestra was playing exactly suited my mood. On the way out, impulse prompted me to cross the dining-room to the dais where the musicians were resting between numbers.

"Gentlemen," I said, "I have thoroughly enjoyed your program. Several of your numbers were particular favorites of mine. And you put so much spirit into your playing. I want to thank you."

5

Their faces broke into smiles, and I left them beaming over their instruments. The rest of my own evening was happier.

*   *   *

One Sunday afternoon I fell to thinking of an elderly gentleman in failing health whom I had not seen for a long time.

"Why not surprise him by calling him up?" I asked myself.

"I was thinking of you and I wanted to have a little chat," I explained when he came to the phone. We had an enjoyable five-minute visit.

His wife told me, a few days later, that my call had done more for him than a whole bottle of his tonic. "You know," she explained, "the telephone almost never rings for him anymore."

*   *   *

Tiny episodes, all of these; but they are collectors' items in my hobby of giving myself away.

You may do such things yourself, quite naturally, without stopping to think of them as "gifts." If so, you are to be congratulated. But, judging from my own experience, I'll wager that you could do more of them, if you would make a real hobby of self-giving. And I'll promise that you'll be happier—in proportion as you give.

Only once in recent years have I violated my giving-away philosophy. In suggesting an idea to a shoe manufacturer I hinted that I would not be averse to receiving a pair of shoes in payment. He liked my idea and sent me a certificate good for any pair of shoes of his manufacture. I selected a smart pair of an expensive last and wore them proudly home.

But I lived to regret my avarice! That particular last was not suited to my foot, and it took my feet months to recover from the damage those shoes did. So now when I give away an idea there isn't even a shoestring attached!

Chapter 3

"A Portion of Thyself"

Ralph Waldo Emerson, that lofty idealist who neverthe-less had a penetratingly practical knowledge of human na-ture, wrote: "Rings and jewels are not gifts, but apologies for gifts. The only gift is a portion of thyself."

Almost anything in the world can be bought for money—except the warm impulses of the human heart. They have to be *given*. And they are priceless in their power to purchase happiness for two people, the recipient and the giver.

Many letters have come to me from people who want to try giving themselves away, but are timid. They are afraid that their simple gifts-of-the-heart would be laughed at. As one correspondent expressed it, "I have nothing of any im-portance to give to anyone."

This is not true. While we may not look upon what we have to offer as being of any particular value, it may fill a need in someone's life. And if it does that, even for a frac-tion of a minute, it will add that much to the world's happi-ness. And happiness is one of the greatest gifts within the power of any of us to bestow, particularly in these troubled days when the world is so full of fear and hatred, and men's minds and hearts are so anxious.

8

There are a hundred ways to give a portion of yourself. But they all start from the same spot—*your heart*. The French have a proverb: "He gives nothing who does not give himself."

"A portion of thyself" will, therefore, be your stock-in-giving if you want to add to the happiness of those around you, and to lead a happier and more exciting life yourself. It is the *spirit*, not the *substance*, which carries warmth.

You need not worry for a second because you lack money or material things. You can give yourself extravagantly if you choose, and reap great happiness from your giving, without reaching for your pocketbook. As Longfellow phrased it, "Give what you have. To someone, it may be better than you dare to think."

✓ ✓ ✓

Indeed, of all the things a person may give, money is probably the least permanent in the pleasure it produces, and the most likely to backfire on the giver. Sometimes it results in resentment, sometimes even in wrecked friendship. If you must give money, bear in mind the wise saying of Miguel de Unamuno y Jugo: "It is not the shilling I give you that counts, but the warmth that it carries with it from my hand."

A New England man stated, "It takes courage to give a small portion of yourself in lieu of some obviously valuable article. But a lively imagination made it possible for me to perceive a great many ways in which I might 'spend myself,' instead of the cash I lacked."

I like the conception of "spending one's self," though I believe that over the years one's *spending* turns out to be *investing*.

Some time ago I received a letter from a woman berating me bitterly for my article on giving-away. She said that her husband was a "giver," that he had given away their money, their food, the children's clothes, and even their household articles, until they were living almost in poverty.

I have no patience with such giving. When it comes to money and material things, I believe the needs of one's family should always come first. A person has no right to give away things which belong to others, even in the name of generosity. This book is about giving *yourself*.

You are trying to give pleasure to someone, and you know from experience what trifling things give you pleasure. Such simple gifts as a compliment on your home or your children or your new hat, a note, a telephone call, or a simple act that reflects thoughtfulness or friendly interest, will set you up for an hour, perhaps for a whole day. They are the truest form of giving, because they come from the heart—they are literally a portion of the giver.

Happiness must be sipped, not drained from life in great gulps. Nor does it flow in a steady stream like water from a faucet.

"A portion of thyself" is a sip of happiness, as satisfying as it is costless.

Chapter 4

Obey Your Warmhearted Impulses

The secret of successfully giving yourself away lies not so much in calculated actions as in cultivating friendly, warmhearted impulses. You have to train yourself to obey giving impulses on the instant—before they get a chance to cool. When you give impulsively, something happens inside of you that makes you glow, sometimes for hours.

Frequently, impulse-giving results in a new friendship, or leads to an interesting adventure. One afternoon during a wartime gas shortage I was driving up a steep hill on my way home. On the sidewalk was a woman carrying two large bags of groceries. My impulse was to stop and ask if she would like a ride. But it meant stopping on the hillside.

"She probably lives on one of the side streets a block or so up the hill," I told myself. But my giving-self squelched that argument and I pulled over to the curb.

"Can I give you a lift?" I asked.

The woman got in gratefully. She had been obliged to walk two miles to the village for her groceries, since the merchants delivered only twice a week and company had descended on her unexpectedly. She was just starting the long trek home with her bundles.

It turned out that she lived just around the corner from my own home, having moved there very recently. Thus, by obeying an impulse, I made the acquaintance of a delightful new neighbor.

⁊ ⁊ ⁊

One evening I was having dinner in a restaurant. The soup was especially good. On impulse I said to the waiter, "Please tell the chef this mushroom soup is delicious."

The waiter looked surprised, then pleased. So, apparently, was the chef, for when the vanilla ice cream I ordered for dessert was served, it was smothered with crushed strawberries, though they were not on the menu. The chef had obeyed an impulse, too—and surprised me!

You just never can tell *what* will happen when you act on a giving impulse!

⁊ ⁊ ⁊

I am sometimes asked, "When you obey your impulses, aren't you likely to be *too* impetuous and get yourself into embarrassing situations?"

Yes; every so often. But what of it? We are supposed to be getting fun out of life. We lose so much by *not* obeying our impulses that I figure we can afford to take a few risks for the sake of adventure.

⁊ ⁊ ⁊

There is a serious aspect to impulse-giving, too. We never know when some impulse action of ours may mean much in the life of a friend or neighbor.

A young dentist of my acquaintance was struggling along

in Boston, trying to build a practice. He had come to the end of his money. One bleak Monday morning in February he decided that he would have to give up his dreams of a professional career in Boston and return to his home town.

That morning one of his friends was passing the brownstone building in which his office was located. At church the previous Sunday he had noticed that the dentist looked depressed. Purely on impulse, he decided to stop in to see him. As he mounted the stairs he met the dentist descending.

"Well, where are you going at this time of the morning?" he demanded cheerily.

The dentist confessed that he was going out to make arrangements to have his equipment shipped to his home town. "I just can't make a go of it here in Boston," he admitted sorrowfully.

Taking the young man by the shoulders, the caller turned him around and marched him upstairs.

"Unlock that door," he commanded. "Turn on the lights—all of them—make this place bright and cheerful. You are not going to give up *now,* after all the months you have invested in this place. Goodbye." And, with a friendly slap on the back, he departed.

✦   ✦   ✦

That afternoon a woman came in who had been recommended to the dentist by a friend. Over a period of weeks this woman's dental work amounted to $300, and her enthusiastic recommendation brought other patients. The tide had turned. In time the man who was saved from quitting by the impulsive act of a friend on a gloomy morning became one of Back Bay's leading dentists.

One day I received this brief note on feminine notepaper from England:

Today I was in the blues. Domestic affairs were a bit worrying. I sat down at my desk to do accounts, but before beginning picked up *The Reader's Digest* and read your article. "Isn't that nice" was my inward exclamation when I had finished. The blues had vanished and I felt quite cheered. You say "one must act fast, while the impulse is fresh." So I am writing at once to send my appreciation.

This woman could not know that her impulsive note from across the Atlantic would arrive at a time when I was going through a period of discouragement, and that it would cheer me as much as my article had cheered her.

Following is another letter which was inspired by that same article:

My first thought, which from long habit I instantly put out of my mind, was to drop you a note telling you how much I enjoyed your article. Then it occurred to me that I was not obeying that natural impulse that made your article so interesting. It also made me realize something that I hadn't really brought to the front of my mind before. I had always thought of certain friends as being generous, but, after thinking it over, I believe they are really successful people at "giving-away."

The writer of this letter has hit on the truth; giving-away is not a matter of generosity—it is really the basis of *successful living*.

✦ ✦ ✦

The late George Matthew Adams, in one of his syndicated newspaper articles, suggested that everyone set aside one day a week as Surprise Day, and do surprising little things for his friends.

Why not *every day?* There are plenty of opportunities for surprise-giving if you look for them.

The great virtue of surprise is that, whereas things people expect have already lost much of their power to give pleasure, the tiniest surprise adds fresh zest to living.

This is what makes impulse-giving so exciting, for both the surpriser and the surprisee.

Chapter 5

A Businessman With a Hobby

Some people may give themselves as an expression of un-selfishness. To others it may be a matter of conscience. Still others may cultivate giving-away as a Christian duty—and surely giving yourself is the heart of the gospel of Christ, who gave himself wholly.

I respect all of these motives. But I took up giving-away as a hobby because I found that it made my life more exciting, and broadened my circle of friends. I became a happier person. While it pleases me that other people are made happier, I do not look upon anything I do for them as being my con-scientious or Christian duty, or as being unselfish. Unselfish-ness for its own sake does not particularly interest me. It is rather a "goody-goody" idea, and smacks of self-righteousness.

But when we take a good look at its opposite—*selfishness*—then unselfishness begins to take on an entirely different aspect. For nobody ever found real and lasting happiness in being completely selfish—not in the whole long history of the world. It seems to be a law of life that we enrich ourselves most when we *give* ourselves most fully and freely.

Selfishness, on the other hand, is a sort of slow poison. One dose leads to another, until the system becomes so saturated with it that one's whole life becomes bitter and disappointing. Larger doses are tried in desperation, but they fail to produce the desired results. The end is disappointment.

Giving-away rids the system of the poisons of selfishness, and produces a healthy glow that warms the spirit.

So I refuse to be considered "unselfish" or "generous" or "self-sacrificing." I am just a businessman with a hobby.

𝘺　𝘺　𝘺

If you are not already an enthusiastic giver-away, perhaps this hobby is just what you need to fill your life with interest and adventure.

If you do take it up in a serious way, let me give you two good starting rules:

First: Never forget that the *little* giving-impulses are as important as the *big* ones—more important in a way, for they help you to form the *habit* of giving yourself away. And until this becomes second nature, your hobby will not pay its fullest dividends.

Second: Start your giving-away as early in the morning as possible. Days are short and the earlier you warm up your spirit and get it "turning over," the more people you will have made happy by the time you tumble into bed at night— and the more exciting your day will have been.

Chapter 6

Bread Upon the Waters

It did not take me long, after I took up giving-away as a hobby, to discover that it is virtually impossible to give yourself away without getting back more than you give— *provided you give away with no thought of any reward.* As Seneca, the Roman philosopher, wrote: "There is no grace in a benefit that sticks to the fingers."

Usually the return comes in some wholly unexpected form, perhaps long after you have forgotten the giving-away episode.

For example, one Sunday morning an important special delivery letter was delivered to my home, though it was addressed to me at my office and the post office would have discharged its obligation by attempting to deliver it there. I wrote the postmaster a note of appreciation.

More than a year later I was in pressing need of a post office box for a new enterprise I was starting. The clerk at the window told me there were no boxes available, that my name would have to go on a long waiting list.

I appealed to the assistant postmaster, who told me the same thing. As I started to leave, keenly disappointed, the postmaster appeared in the doorway of his adjoining office.

He had overheard the conversation and my name had caught his ear.

"Are you the David Dunn who wrote us that nice letter a year or so ago about our delivering a special delivery to your home one Sunday morning?" I said I was.

"Well, you don't know what a letter like that means to us. We usually get nothing but kicks. You are certainly going to have a box in this post office if we have to *make* one for you."

A few days later I had a box. Bread upon the waters!

✦ ✦ ✦

Without thought of reward, a woman in Alexandria, Virginia, acted on a giving-impulse when a young friend had measles. Realizing that the little girl would be cooped up for some days, she wrote her a series of whimsical letters which she illustrated with clever drawings. Instead of using her own name, she signed the letters "Susie Cucumber," the name of a little fox terrier loved by the neighborhood children.

When she recovered from the measles, the little girl told her friends about the Susie Cucumber letters. Immediately they all wished "Susie" would write to them. Parents, grandparents, uncles, and aunts gladly paid for a series of letters. Soon this woman was doing a profitable business on a subscription basis, sending out as many as 100,000 letters a year to children all over the world. A wholly unexpected return on an investment in giving-away.

✦ ✦ ✦

In a letter published in *The Reader's Digest*, R. Webber, Jr. tells of being so impressed with the courtesy of a conductor toward the passengers on a Chicago bus that he spoke to him about it when the crowd had thinned out.

"Well," explained the conductor, "about five years ago I read in the paper about a man who was included in a will just because he was polite. 'What the heck,' I thought, 'it might happen to me.' So I started treating passengers like people. And it makes me feel so good that now I don't care if I never get a million dollars!"

That is exactly what I have discovered! Doing what you can to make life more livable for other people makes your own life fuller. Friends multiply and good things come to you from every direction. The world has a way of balancing accounts with givers-away—provided their hands aren't outstretched for return favors.

✸ ✸ ✸

In this matter of bread returning on the waters, one reader of this book took me to task for even mentioning such a possibility. "It takes all of the virtue out of your giving philosophy," he wrote.

I cheerfully admitted to this correspondent that to give *expecting* a return is not true giving. But to enjoy the unexpected dividends that come to one along the way is to honor the philosophy, for it means that others are experiencing a happy glow in giving to you. And we should learn to accept graciously just as we must be gracious in our giving-away.

Actually, we must *lose ourselves* in our giving-away in order to find true and enduring happiness. This means that we must rise above self-consciousness. After all, self-consciousness is just another term for self-centeredness. It means that we are putting *ourselves* first in our thoughts and feelings, and letting everyone else come second. This is not practicing good will, but working for a reward.

There is no self-consciousness in good will. It flows from our hearts, naturally and spontaneously, without calculated forethought. It expresses itself in understanding and tolerance and a desire to share with others without thought of any return.

This discovery explained to me why some of the readers of this book who had accepted its philosophy were having trouble making it "work." Their giving-away was self-conscious. Being self-conscious, they were overly sensitive to the reactions of the recipients of their little kindnesses. Quite unconsciously, it led them to expect some sort of thanks or gratitude. If this was not forthcoming, or if they sensed an attitude of either suspicion toward their motives or cynical indifference, they retreated inside themselves to lick their wounds.

At first I reacted this way myself to the occasional rebuffs I received. I felt disappointed in people and was discouraged in my giving-away impulses for days, sometimes weeks.

This self-conscious reaction is not unnatural. Usually it means that, quite unconsciously, we are really thinking of ourselves, and expecting our happiness to come from outside ourselves. Whereas the miracle of happiness must originate within us.

✓   ✓   ✓

Some people give for the long future rather than the immediate present. Thomas Dreier tells the story of a man over eighty who was observed by a neighbor to be planting a small peach tree:

"Do you expect to eat peaches from that tree?" the neighbor asked.

The old gentleman rested on his spade. "No," he said. "At my age I know I won't. But all my life I've enjoyed peaches —never from a tree I had planted myself. I wouldn't have had peaches if other men hadn't done what I'm doing now. I'm just trying to pay the other fellows who planted peach trees for me."

In practicing giving-away we both plant peach trees and eat peaches, often unconscious of the fruits of our own little thoughtfulnesses, and equally of the thoughtfulnesses others have invested for our benefit, perhaps many years ago.

Today's giving-away is a blind investment in future happiness, though we can never tell when, where, or in what form this happiness will come.

Which is part of the fun!

Chapter 7

Giving Yourself "In Kind"

There is a trade term—"in kind"—which applies in a special sense to giving-away. In the old days a farmer might pay his bill at the general store "in kind," that is, in some produce he had raised. Or he might pay his taxes, not in cash, but in hours of labor, working on the township roads.

A gift of ourselves "in kind"—something we can *make* or *do*—is often more acceptable to people than anything we might buy for them. We are inclined to value too lightly the gifts in kind which we have to offer our friends, neighbors, and fellow workers. We take our talents too much for granted.

Within each of us is a great store of giveable riches. It may be in the form of skill of hand, or of some special proficiency or training. It may be the ability to entertain, to organize, to teach. It may be a talent that we have never taken seriously, but which might be cultivated for the pleasure of others. Or it may be a surplus of time.

Failing any of these, what we have to give may be just warmth of heart—and if we think of our heart rather than our purse as the reservoir of our giving, we shall find it full all the time!

A gift in kind is truly a gift of a portion of oneself.

One Christmas there arrived at our home a box from a farm family. We knew this family lived near no city where they could shop for Christmas gifts. What had they sent us?

Upon opening the box on Christmas morning we found twelve pint jars of home-canned farm products—kernel corn, wax beans, tender little beets, squash, lamb stew, mince meat. No present we received that Christmas was as much appreciated as those twelve pint jars, all neatly labeled in the handwriting of the farmer's wife. They were a gift of herself and her hard-working husband.

✓ ✓ ✓

A fine example of giving one's craftsmanship is the story of A. E. Shaw, a manufacturer of gavels, from Rocky River, Ohio, as told in a newspaper story at the time the United Nations was being organized:

"I was listening on the radio to the closing session of the United Nations Conference when Stettinius wound it up," Mr. Shaw related. "He pounded the gavel one, two, three times. The first time it sounded all right, but the third time I said to myself, 'That gavel's done for.'"

On a giving-impulse, Shaw wrote Stettinius offering to make him a new gavel. The offer was accepted. The maker of gavels then put his art and his heart into the fashioning of a very fine gavel. He literally gave himself in kind to the United Nations.

✓ ✓ ✓

Most physicians, even the famous specialists who command high fees, give their services to deserving people who are unable to pay for medical or surgical care. From others who are well able to pay, they exact substantial fees. In this way they balance their giving in kind with their professional getting.

It has always seemed to me that this balancing idea is both wise and fair. I have no patience with so-called "generous" people who give their time and talents so prodigally that they are a worry to their relatives and friends because they do not earn enough to support themselves and their families. That is unsound giving in kind.

And in the present state of world confusion and strife, nothing—but nothing—could be a more appreciated gift to all humanity than a surge of giving in kind by each and every one of us.

✶ ✶ ✶

We are not all physicians, but many of us earn our living with some talent, skill, or craft which we can share on a balanced getting-and-giving basis, charging the world a self-respecting price for our services, but giving ourselves freely in kind to worthy causes and deserving individuals who need our help.

Emerson was referring to gifts in kind when he wrote, ". . . Therefore the poet brings his poem; the shepherd, his lamb; the farmer, corn; the miner, a gem; the sailor, coral and shells; the painter, his picture; the girl, a handkerchief of her own sewing."

After all, what gift could be so appropriate as a bit of one's own skill of hand or mind?

"You do not have to be rich to be generous," wrote Corinne U. Wells. "If he has the spirit of true generosity, a pauper can give like a prince."

Each of us withholds every day a score of little gifts in kind that could make our small personal world, and by multiplication the whole big world, a happier place.

Chapter 8

Minutes and Hours Make Fine Gifts

Each of us receives an equal allotment of time—twenty-four hours every day of the year. Even the busiest among us has from a few minutes to an hour or more a day which he could give to others in the form of some useful service. Opportunities for time-giving are to be found all around us.

Many of us have a knack at something. If we were to use it in our spare time to do things for other people, we would be giving something that perhaps no one else in the world could give quite so acceptably.

A Boston businessman who was very fond of children but had none of his own used to stop in at a small home for orphans every Wednesday afternoon between five and six o'clock and entertain the youngsters, giving the matron and her helpers an hour of complete freedom.

He was a big, solemn-faced man, but the children saw right through his dignity. The instant he arrived in the playroom they gathered around him with shouts of joy. In his pocket he would have a bag of hard candy, a packet of picture cards, or some penny trinkets—always just one for each child, which made it all the more precious. Squatting on the floor, he would distribute his treasures, then launch into a story.

He was known to the youngsters as The Big Man, for he had stipulated to the matron that his name should be withheld. He wanted none of his business associates to know of his hour with these orphans. "They would think me a sentimental old fool," he explained.

In that hour each week he gave great happiness to a group of fatherless and motherless youngsters, and welcome relief to three overburdened women. "But nobody gets the fun out of it that I do," he always insisted.

He is now dead, but the many boys and girls whose lives he brightened over the years will never lose the memory of The Big Man who gave them an hour of himself every Wednesday, and along with that hour some of his fine character.

Yet many of us would ask, "What really worthwhile giving of myself could I do in one hour a week?"

✓ ✓ ✓

A retired railroad engineer with time on his hands tends store every day from twelve to one o'clock in a small neighborhood grocery run by a widow who has two small children. While she prepares lunch for her children, he indulges a lifelong ambition to run a grocery store.

"It's the most fun of any hour of my day," he declares. "And handling food for an hour makes me so ravenous that I enjoy my own lunch just about twice as much!"

The truth is, his lunch is seasoned with the spice of giving!

✓ ✓ ✓

An elderly woman of my acquaintance, herself a grandmother, goes every pleasant morning to a certain bench in a city park and watches over from three to half a dozen baby carriages, while the babies' grateful mothers shop or get a hairdo.

✓ ✓ ✓

Another woman in my neighborhood has "adopted" an old lady in a nearby home for the aged. She calls on her once a week, writes her notes between visits, remembers her birthday, takes her and some of her cronies for occasional automobile rides, and loans her books. All in two or three hours a week.

There are many old people and invalids and children in institutions, whose lives would be brightened immeasurably if someone would "adopt" them.

✓ ✓ ✓

We are prone to think we have no time to give away if we cannot bank on having spare hours. No matter; even minutes, usefully invested, are precious gifts.

When our country was at war one of the busiest women of my acquaintance kept a steady stream of letters flowing to many service men from her suburban community, whether she knew them well or not. She wrote them the news of their home town, and told them of the doings of the younger set, which she picked up from her own children at mealtime.

Knowing of her strenuous program of war activities, which involved almost daily trips to the city, I marveled at the volume of her G.I. correspondence. One morning I happened to ride to the city with her and she showed me her secret. Opening her handbag, she exhibited a packet of note sheets and stamped envelopes, a fountain pen, and a list of G.I.'s names and service addresses.

"Whenever I have to wait, even four or five minutes, for

a train or an appointment, I address an envelope and start a note," she explained. "Once started, it is easy to add another paragraph the next time I have a few minutes. I average half a dozen letters a day, with seldom as many as ten uninterrupted minutes. And you should see the letters that come back!

"I hesitated to start writing to the boys," she went on to explain, "for fear the things I wrote about would not interest them. But they gave me plenty to write about!"

This last statement has great significance to the would-be giver who lacks imagination as to what he or she may have to give to others. If you *start* to give yourself, be it in ever so simple a fashion, the world will observe your spirit and show you many needs that you can supply.

There are a hundred ways of giving away little margins of time you never will miss, which could be riches to someone.

✓   ✓   ✓

I know a busy executive who dictates many letters. Each morning he formulates a short paragraph of personal news or comment outside the realm of business which he has his secretary add, with appropriate variations, to nearly all his letters for the day. As a result, his correspondence has a warmth and friendliness rare in the business world. Yet not a minute of his busy office day does this take, for he formulates the daily paragraph—a bit of himself—on the way to the city on his suburban train.

✓   ✓   ✓

Oddly enough—or perhaps naturally—the busiest people are apt to do the best job of giving-away. They are so busy that they have to obey their giving-impulses *promptly,* and get on with their affairs. Whereas people with plenty of time are likely to debate within themselves: "Shall I, or shan't I?" By the time the debate is over, the opportunity has passed.

✦   ✦   ✦

It is so easy to confuse our daily busyness with our daily business. Many of us earn our living in business, but waste much of the rest of our time on busyness that profits us little.

Time was not created merely to be consumed in working and worrying, rushing for trains, and dashing to appointments. It was intended to be used in "the pursuit of happiness," as our discerning forefathers phrased it in the Declaration of Independence. True, we would find it hard to be happy if we did not work, and earn enough to live on. But beyond that, the aim of all of us should be to both *give* and *get* the greatest possible enjoyment from every sixty seconds of our lives.

In terms of downright happiness, it is my experience that the returns-per-minute from *giving* are far greater than the returns from *getting.*

Chapter 9

Truly Great Time-givers

There are today in every community outstanding men and women who are exceedingly generous givers of their time in special services to their fellow citizens, often in very difficult assignments. It is with this group of time-givers that this chapter is concerned.

It is comparatively easy for comfortably fixed citizens to give generously of their money. And of course this is essential to the carrying on of good works and the support of worthy causes. It is less easy but sometimes even more important for able and influential citizens to give many hours of their *time* to the welfare of their communities, and to the solutions of their serious problems.

Many of the problems facing our cities, towns, and suburban communities are so complex, and in some instances so stubborn, that the conventional machinery of local government can hardly cope with them. Nor can the regular social agencies—the churches, schools, boards of education, and the like.

The result is that, increasingly, private citizens of broad experience and exceptional competence are being called upon to head up emergency projects or to undertake difficult community or regional assignments, often at a very great sacrifice of their time and energy and their personal interests.

As I have talked with some of the broad-spirited citizens who have taken on these volunteer assignments, I have come to realize that some of their undertakings are so baffling that no one, no matter how courageous or conscientious, can be certain of success.

The citizen who shoulders such responsibilities needs a personal philosophy that he can put on like a cloak to keep his spirit warm and protect it from the setbacks and discouragements he may expect to encounter.

"It takes a special kind of personal philosophy to carry a man through a job such as you have taken on," I remarked to one friend who had just assumed the chairmanship of a particularly tough assignment in the area of local race relations.

"Just what kind of a philosophy?" he asked.

"I think of it as a simple giving-philosophy," said I. "Instead of worrying about whether you might fall short of your objectives, or even fail, you make up your mind that you will concentrate on *giving yourself* to the task, wholeheartedly:

Your time
Your experience
Your special abilities
Your influence
Your understanding and your tolerance
Your good will
Your courage and your faith

"This is quite a packet of gifts, but each gift is important. Together they put the emphasis where it belongs: on what you can *give* to the task, not on how tough the job is. If you give everything you possibly can, you will have done your citizenship best. No one could do more."

"I like that idea!" he exclaimed. "It is as sound psychologically as it is generous in its spirit. And one can have the comfortable knowledge that if he does fall short of his aims he has given his very best."

Such a giving-philosophy is likely to be contagious. Those associating with a leader so motivated are likely to start giving themselves in the same broad spirit, which begets both dedication and confidence.

✓ ✓ ✓

Meanwhile, each of us can contribute to the success of these selfless givers-away in our own communities. For we in our turn can give to them our cooperation, our appreciation, our encouragement, our faith.

And no matter how able, important, or influential a citizen may be, these gifts from his fellow townsmen will mean everything to him as he meets the problems and discouragements of the project he has undertaken.

Chapter 10

Giving Away One's Retirement

"What about the steadily growing army of retired business and professional men?" I am sometimes asked. "Couldn't nearly all of them give of their time and experience in some useful way?"

Indeed they could. And many of them do.

For example, a retired chain store executive of my acquaintance, who has plenty of time on his hands, put himself at the disposal of the Women's Club of his resort city to give informal talks to audiences of housewives on how to get the most for their money when shopping.

This man knows merchandise, and he knows women and their shopping habits. In an hour's time he shows them many practical ways to save money, and to get more for the money they do spend. After half an hour's talk he throws the meeting open to questions. Invariably the sessions end up with expressions of deep appreciation from the women, who say that they never realized how easy it could be to get better value for their money.

Also, invariably the speaker has a thoroughly enjoyable time dusting off and using his accumulated marketing experience.

In today's world, with its welter of troublesome problems and its beckoning opportunities, any experienced business or professional man will be doing both himself and his times a great service if he will accept—or perhaps actually seek out —local, state, and national projects or programs where his experience and abilities can be put to work usefully.

A retired man in any community who is a good organizer might even multiply himself by calling together a group of retirees. They could make an informal survey of the needs of the people of their community (or region) and set up a clearing house for studying and supplying these needs, with voluntary contributions of time and experience, not only by retired citizens, but by local organizations and public-spirited citizens. This sort of retirement-giving is sorely needed today in many communities.

The fact is, no retired man needs to be bored. He has but to find—or to use his imagination or resourcefulness to create —useful ways to give away his retirement.

Chapter 11

Multiply Little Gifts by Three

You can, if you will, multiply the acceptability of thoughtful little gifts by three.

The first multiplier is the *friendly spirit* of your giving. Nearly always the spirit is more important than the gift itself. If it comes from your heart, whether it be a simple "thank you," an enthusiastic note of congratulation, a tumbler of homemade jelly, or a compliment to your secretary, it is more acceptable than a costly present given grudgingly or from a sense of duty—which nearly always can be felt by the recipient. The spirit is *you*—"a portion of thyself," as Emerson expressed it.

The second multiplier is the *timeliness* of the gift. Too often we let the moment pass when it is within our power to give some person happiness. A day, an hour, even a few minutes later, the same action will have lost its keen edge of pleasure. That is why impulse-giving has so much to commend it. Your mind and heart take in the situation as it exists at a particular moment in the lives of the people concerned. Your action is tailored to the situation, making it not only well-timed but appropriate.

The third—and most potent—multiplier is *enthusiasm.*

37

One reason we get so little excitement out of our daily lives is because we put so little enthusiasm into our hourly living. Whenever we meet a person who is genuinely enthusiastic, it gives us a lift. Such people are givers-of-themselves and are welcome wherever they go, because they make life more interesting. Each of us can do the same for other people.

It takes no great effort, but merely thoughtfulness, to put enthusiasm into your voice in giving-away. When you add enthusiasm, you give people double pleasure, for so few of us put our hearts and eyes and voices into our dealings with those around us. We seem to take it for granted that words are all that are necessary, but words carry only a small part of what we say. The tone in which we say them, if it conveys the warmth of our personality, is much more important than our words.

✦ ✦ ✦

Some of us are undemonstrative because we don't want to be thought "gushers." But it is not necessary to be a gusher to be enthusiastic. People who pride themselves on taking everything and everybody matter-of-factly, assuming that other people understand how they feel, would be surprised to find how cold and unappreciative they are thought to be by all but their closest friends—who know what they are like underneath.

One man of my acquaintance, who took great satisfaction in never "gushing," told me that at forty-five he was shocked to find that his philosophy of appreciation had been wrong.

"I felt so deeply appreciative for the things people did for me that I was sure they must feel my appreciation," he explained. "But one day I did not get a promotion I had supposed was coming to me. I asked why another man had been chosen for the higher job and was told it was because my superiors thought I silently disapproved of everything and everybody, and with such an attitude I could not be a leader. I investigated further and found that all but my closest friends thought of me as a wet blanket because I never *enthused* over anything."

This man was an absorber of appreciation, but gave none in return because of a misguided sense of reserve.

✓ ✓ ✓

Here is good news for those to whom enthusiasm does not come naturally: *It can be cultivated.*

At first you must consciously put your eyes, your voice, your spirit—in a word, *yourself*—into your appreciation of people and events and things. Do this around your home, at your work, and in your social contacts, and you will be surprised how quickly it will become second nature. You will find yourself living in a more gracious and enthusiastic world, for your enthusiasm will be reflected back to you from the people to whom you give it.

Spirit, Timeliness, Enthusiasm. These are the three Great Multipliers. They form an important part of the art of giving-away.

Chapter 12

The Unbuyable Gifts

Consider the simple gifts that money cannot buy, such as kindness, thoughtfulness, courtesy, consideration, and good nature.

Do not misunderstand me: I do not advocate developing a Pollyanna personality. It is just good manners and good sense to be courteous, thoughtful, kindly, considerate, and good-natured.

Take kindness, for example. One night a good many years ago as a Lackawanna ferry nosed into its slip at Hoboken, the passengers in the cabin crowded toward the door—all but one man who was slouched in a drunken sleep.

Perhaps twenty people glanced at the drunkard as they passed. Then one old gentleman went out of his way to step over and shake the sleeper. "Hoboken," he shouted in the man's ear in a kindly tone.

A dozen people turned at the sound of the voice. A look of shame crept into their faces as the whispered word went around that the man who had thought to do what any one of them might have done was Thomas Edison.

"It never occurred to me until I read *Try Giving Yourself Away* that one could adopt simple *kindliness* as a giving-away hobby," wrote one reader.

Why not? Not only is it a fine hobby, but it is a wonderful way to collect friends. Because it springs *from* the heart and speaks *to* the heart.

✓ ✓ ✓

So, also, does *considerateness*.

Doubtless you are a normally considerate person. I had thought of myself as such. But I was surprised to discover how much *more* considerate I could be by cultivating the habit of projecting my mind, for a tiny fraction of a second, into the mind and heart of every person I encountered. This technique revealed an astonishing number of opportunities to say something or do something that would make some person warmly appreciative.

You can even be considerate silently. A train starts to fill up. Instead of spreading out over the seat to try to keep it to yourself, you can make the vacant space beside you look inviting. You will find yourself enjoying your spirit of sharing as much as it is appreciated by the fellow passenger who settles beside you in response to your silent hospitality.

✓ ✓ ✓

Thoughtfulness is a twin of considerateness.

One of the busiest and most successful professional men in America is the most thoughtful person I have ever known. Just to come into his presence is to experience a sense of being looked after, so many are the little things he does and says that make you feel comfortable, in mind and body. I verily believe that from the time this man gets up in the morning until he goes to bed at night, he never neglects an opportunity to exercise thoughtfulness, with his family, his patients, his professional associates, his friends, and the strangers he encounters. Yet no one would think of accusing this man of being saccharine. He is not the gushy type; in fact his personality is a bit on the austere side. But he is loved and respected by all who come in contact with him.

✓ ✓ ✓

Courage is one of the really rare gifts.

How often, in a group or a meeting, do we see some man or woman take a courageous stand in a situation where a hard decision is required, with the result that the whole group decides aright.

Some years ago there passed away a member of a board of directors on which I was serving. The president of the board paid him this fine tribute: "In all the years Walter served on this board, whenever there was a decision to be made which took courage, he always faced the issue, no matter how unpleasant or unpopular it might be, and insisted that we make the *right* decision. He literally *gave* courage to all of us."

The person who gives his courage indeed gives a worthy gift to his fellowmen, and to the world at large.

✓ ✓ ✓

Good nature is a gift which brightens the world and reflects back on the giver.

Several years ago a very wealthy man declared that he would give a million dollars for one of his associate's quick, good-natured smiles. Yet he might have had it for nothing had he but schooled himself to smile in every trying situation —and charge it up to good nature. For a warm, friendly smile is appropriate to any situation. It is a sample of what you are in your heart, so you are literally giving a bit of *yourself.*

A friend who journeyed around the world before the days of world cruises, when native peoples were not used to tourists, told me, "A smile was the one thing the people of every country understood. So I smiled myself around the globe, and made friends in every country—without the services of an interpreter!"

In my own more limited travels abroad I have found that a smile given to waiters, porters, railway conductors, hotel clerks, and shopkeepers, works magic in the lands where language is a barrier.

In the present upset condition of the world we shall make little progress toward peace and friendly relations until nations stop scowling at each other and begin to exchange friendly smiles. And that will come when they stop trying so hard to *get,* and do a little *giving.*

Years ago I encountered a legend that I have never forgotten: "Good nature begets smiles, smiles beget friends, and friends are better than a fortune."

✓   ✓   ✓

Perhaps you have never thought of the simple things mentioned in this chapter as gifts. That is our trouble: We think of a gift as something that can be bought, something material that can be seen and handled. Whereas the heart has its own method of weighing and measuring, and its own scale of values.

Chapter 13

The Getters and the Givers

One noon I was lunching with a friend in an ultrafashionable New York hotel.

"Look at these people around us," he said. "Undoubtedly they are among the world's most successful getters. Most of them look as though they have plenty of money. Probably many of them occupy high positions in the social world. Do you see many faces that look really happy?"

We both studied the faces of the people at every table within eye-range. Few of them did look happy. At two tables the people were laughing, but it was artificial, not the spontaneous laughter of people in a really happy mood.

We were merely re-observing something I had noticed over the years: that as a rule the gathering places of the most successful getters are seldom wholesomely happy spots. Too often the "happiness" is provided by professional entertainers.

✓ ✓ ✓

The trouble is, so many of the people who are outstandingly successful at getting are too self-centered to be truly happy. There are notable exceptions, of course. Here and

44

there you will see a getting person whose face advertises a happy spirit. When you do, if you watch that person closely you will nearly always find that he is gracious, considerate of the people who are serving him, and more concerned about the happiness and well-being of his companions than he is of his own comfort.

Such people are natural sharers, and those around them neither envy nor resent their good fortune, for they are givers as well as getters.

But the more I watch the men and women who have been markedly successful in getting, the more I am impressed with the fact that as a general rule it is the givers who are the genuinely happy people.

*   *   *

At first I was inclined to be critical of the confirmed getters, who seem always to think first of *their* interests, *their* pleasure, *their* rights, *their* welfare. But the more I have observed them—and earnestly tried to give to them a measure of tolerant understanding—the more clearly I have come to realize that their self-centeredness is not a matter of deliberate choice.

Some people are born with a tendency to worry; others with a cheerful, optimistic outlook on life. Some are born with an acquisitive faculty; others with no knack at making money. Some are born with a love for art, music, or poetry; others with no taste for these graces.

Just so, some people are born with a giving spirit; others are born with a getting spirit, or else they are raised in an environment where getting is the aim and end of life. In the case of the latter group, it is not their fault; rather it is their misfortune, for unless they take positive steps to overcome it they are likely to lose out on that happiness of spirit which is the finest fruit of living.

✐ ✐ ✐

When I came to this realization, I began to try especially hard to give of myself to the getters in my circle of friends and acquaintances. Then, one day, it came over me that my motive was not completely unselfish. I was really trying to make them feel ashamed of themselves.

"Certainly that is not the proper spirit in which to give to them," I told myself. "I am being smug. And smugness has no place in anyone's giving-away."

At this juncture I stumbled upon a practical way of giving to the naturally selfish people I knew. I suggested to them little things they could do that would be gifts-of-themselves, thus "sampling" the fun of giving-away.

For example, one of my most self-centered friends made a favorable comment to me about an article written by a mutual friend:

"Why don't you drop him a note and tell him just what you told me?" I asked. "It would give him a real lift." Rather to my surprise, he did, and the next time I saw him he beamingly showed me an appreciative note he had received from the man. That little episode opened a new door to happiness for a natural getter.

✐ ✐ ✐

Another self-centered friend received a big box of Temple oranges from a relative in Florida. He remarked that since Temple oranges did not keep well they would probably spoil before he and his wife could possibly eat all of them.

"Why don't you bring a bag of four of those delicious oranges to each of the four people in your office?" I asked him.

The next morning he left four bags of oranges on the front seat of his car in the company's parking lot, and told each of the four people to pick up the bag with his or her name on it when they went to their own cars in the evening. The next day the atmosphere around his office was so warm and friendly that he called up on the telephone to tell me how appreciative the four recipients had been.

"I've never done anything like that before in my life," he said rather apologetically. "It certainly made a hit!" He was so pleased that I briefly explained my simple giving-away philosophy and sent him a copy of my book.

This man has since become an enthusiastic giver-away. I am particularly happy to have made a giver of him for it started a chain reaction. He so enjoyed giving away sixteen Temple oranges that ever since he has been busy actively "selling" the giving-away philosophy to his getter friends, some of whom are as self-centered as he was before he discovered what fun giving can be.

Chapter 14

The Priceless Gift of Tolerance

When he was president of Harvard, Dr. Charles W. Eliot delivered a lecture* in which he made this statement: "An honorable man must be generous, and I do not mean generous with money only. I mean generous in his judgments of men and women."

This all sums up in a single word—*tolerance*.

Of all the gifts we can bestow on our friends and neighbors, and upon every person we encounter in our daily goings and comings, none is perhaps so rare as the gift of tolerance. It is as easy to be intolerant, critical, and faultfinding toward people as it is difficult to be fair and tolerant.

Any of us can make tolerance a definite part of our giving-away hobby. To do so calls for action of the heart and mind. The heart says, "Wait, before you judge, until you know *why* this person acts or lives as he or she does." The mind sets out to discover what is beneath the surface, and refuses to sit in judgment until all the facts are known.

Were other people to know the truth behind our own lives, certainly they would judge us more charitably. If we knew

* *The Durable Satisfactions of Life*, (New York: Thomas Y. Crowell Company, 1910).

what people said about us, and how unfair many of their judgments were, I am sure we would be slower to judge others without knowing all that was going on behind the scenes in their lives. Since we do not know, why should we not bestow on them the priceless gift of tolerance, in our thoughts and in talking about them with others, or in listening to others talk about them? It costs us nothing and may be the most wonderful gift we could possibly give them.

✶ ✶ ✶

A man living in a suburb of Boston was for years harshly criticized by his neighbors for attitudes and actions which were certainly hard to condone. He was tolerated socially only because of his charming wife. She was accepted by everyone, and had the sympathy of the entire community because she had to live with such a husband—a boorish, unsociable man who drank too much.

Quite suddenly one day the couple moved away, without even leaving an address with their friends. At a neighborhood bridge party the evening following their departure the unpopular husband received a particularly vicious tearing apart. It was just like him to move away without even saying good-bye. Everybody agreed that it was good riddance to the community, except that his attractive wife would be greatly missed.

Only one person in the neighborhood, a quiet young lawyer, had always declined to be drawn into these discussions, and this evening he kept noticeably aloof from the conversation. Suddenly one of the most outspoken of the women turned on him. "Bradley," she snapped, "you'd think from the way you've never said a word when we've discussed Jim So-and-So that you approved of him."

"I'm afraid I do," he replied. "More, at least, than I approve the way we have torn him apart all these years. Have we ever asked ourselves *why* he has acted as he has? What have we really *known* about his life?"

The prompt and rather ill-natured consensus was that they had known "plenty." The attitude of the lawyer was resented.

He waited for the fire of their spite to die down. Then he said quietly, "I learned in law school not to form judgments until I had the facts. It took me a long time to get the facts in this case, and I've had to keep them to myself until tonight. But now that these people have moved away I'd better let you have them, as I got them from a lawyer friend who works for a Boston detective agency.

"The gracious wife of our unpopular departed neighbor is a confirmed kleptomaniac. She has been caught shoplifting in every large store in the city. Her husband managed to keep her out of jail, usually at a heavy price. He nearly went to jail on one occasion by drawing suspicion to himself. He dreaded to have parties at his home because his wife has been known to steal things from her guests." (Two women in the group exchanged startled glances with their husbands.) "And he tried to keep her from coming to our parties whenever he could because she has been known to take things from other guests' handbags."

The whole group gasped.

It was this experience that really taught me tolerance—to reserve judgment on people until I had the facts, and meanwhile to try to *like* them.

I once read a Sioux Indian's prayer which impressed me deeply: "Great Spirit, help me never to judge another until I have walked two weeks in his moccasins."

Probably the most precious thing a man or woman can possess is a good name. The curious part of it is, scarcely a day passes that we do not have an opportunity to give someone a good name.

Any time we find ourselves in a group of people who are talking about a friend or neighbor or fellow worker, if someone starts to disparage, we can so easily say something kind, or at least tolerant. It is surprising how often this will cause another to speak up and add something favorable to what we have said. Many a time the conversation will end by giving a good name to the person under discussion. When this happens everybody in the group feels better.

Is there not the best authority in the world for tolerance? The Bible says, "Judge not that ye be not judged."

Chapter 15

A Wonderful New Word

Sometimes in the progress of mankind a new word comes along which the world has long needed. This chapter is about such a word, a word which sums up the philosophy of this little book in seven letters.

At the time the original article which grew into this little book was published in *The Reader's Digest,* this word was practically unknown. It will not be found in the twelve volumes of the 1933 edition of the authoritative Oxford Dictionary. But it does appear in the thirteenth supplementary volume of that dictionary. It had just come over the horizon!

The word is *empathy.* Even yet it has only begun to be defined. The best definition I have been able to piece together on my own is: *Entering into the feelings or needs of others; putting yourself in their place; being sympathetic to their troubles, problems, frustrations and sorrows—and rejoicing with them in their good fortune.*

✓ ✓ ✓

Empathy expresses itself in giving of ourselves imagina

tively and spontaneously, in a hundred ways, big and little. I have come to think of it as "empathy-giving."

One of the happy things about empathy-giving is that it fits into the warp and woof of our daily living. We can give the deepest sympathy to those in great trouble, or express our empathy in many small ways.

As an example of the latter, one morning I was in a line at the ticket window in our suburban station. There had been an increase in the price of a special one-day round-trip ticket to the city, from $2.00 to $2.60. This was announced on a conspicious placard right beside the ticket window. In spite of this, each one of the five people ahead of me had to have the whole thing explained to them, and each protested the increase, in spite of the fact that the agent had nothing to do with it.

The agent was patient, but understandably a bit irritated. I had a sudden feeling of empathy for him. When my turn came I said, "Two-sixty New York, please." And laid down exactly $2.60.

"Mister," he said, looking up in pleased surprise, "*you* make my job easy." We grinned at each other understandingly.

A tiny incident, this. But are not our days made up of just such fleeting contacts which often can be oiled with a drop of empathy?

✓   ✓   ✓

It is surprising how quickly this new word is catching on, particularly with the young people. They seem instinctively to understand it. It expresses the idealism of youth. But there is nothing new about this idealism. Back in the early 1920's, before "empathy" was in the dictionaries, one of the young men in H. G. Well's book *Tono-Bungay* is quoted as saying, "I did not want simply to live or simply to live happily or well; I wanted to serve and do and make—with some nobility. It was in me. It is in half the youth of the world."

In spite of the youthful turmoil of our own times the spirit of empathy is stirring many of our young men and women deeply. Indeed, probably it is responsible for some of the turmoil. They are striving to break out of the mold of selfishness, and broaden their spirit of service to their fellows.

✔   ✔   ✔

Another example of empathy is the idea brought out by Joanne Woodward in *The Long Hot Summer* when she says, "I have got a lot to give someone." The implication is that she has been storing up something to give. I believe all of us are storing up giving-impulses all the time, but do too much storing and not enough giving. Sometimes it backs up on us and produces a sense of frustration.

I have proved to myself that we cannot be empathetic without getting more in return than we give. Always provided that we are not holding out our hand. Usually the return comes from some surprising direction, or in some utterly unexpected form. Which adds to the fun!

A very broad principle underlies empathy-giving: When we live narrowly unto ourselves, we have only one person working for us. When we are habitually thoughtful of others, a great many people are working and pulling for us.

The individual who embraces the philosophy of empathy

is developing his own character; building on his own best instincts and impulses. He is bound to become a better, bigger, stronger, finer, happier person. More observing. More thoughtful. More considerate. More mature. More lovable.

Chapter 16

Postage-Stamp Giving

For a few pennies the United States Government will co-operate with you wholeheartedly in one of the simplest and most acceptable forms of giving yourself.

All you have to do is write a note to a friend or acquaintance (or even a stranger) expressing interest, friendship, sympathy, congratulations, commendation, good will, or good wishes; seal it up in an envelope; address it; stick a postage stamp on it; and drop it in the nearest mailbox.

We fail to make greater use of this governmental partnership-in-giving, not because we are unaware of its possibilities, but because we permit ourselves to be thoughtless. We know how much we appreciate notes from friends, but we do not stop often enough to think how much they would appreciate notes from us.

Or perhaps it is procrastination. We promise ourselves on many occasions to write to people, to tell them of our pleasure in something they have done or some honor that has come to them, or to express sympathy for a sorrow. We keep putting it off until some morning we say to ourselves, "Well, it's too late now. I'm sorry I didn't do it when I first thought of it."

Which is just another argument for acting on our little giving-impulses.

There is something peculiarly *you* in the letter or note you write. It says, "I think enough of you to take the trouble to sit down and try to put into words the interest I have in you."

It matters not whether you have the gift of expression. If you say what is in your heart, the words will not matter. And who knows, your letter may arrive at a time of crisis. The course of many a person's life has been changed by a letter received in the morning mail.

A few pennies is a small investment to make in giving ourselves to our friends, or in winning the friendship of strangers who have done something which earns our gratitude or approval.

Chapter 17

On Lowering the One-in-Ten Average

Though the term "giving thanks" has been in use for cen turies, we seem not to think of thanks as a gift. Yet it *is* a gift, for every time you give thanks you give a bit of the warmth of your heart.

I have had people thank me for little thoughtfulnesses with such genuine gratitude in their voices that it has warmed me to the marrow of my bones. Undoubtedly you have had the same experience. Yet how often do we give others all the happiness we might for the things they do for us?

To realize how short we are falling we have only to note the number of times we feel that the thoughtful things we do for other people do not receive quite the thanks we antic ipated.

Our thoughtlessness cannot be blamed entirely on our busy age. The fault is as old as humanity. Christ encountered it in His day. We read in Luke's Gospel:

And it came to pass, as he went to Jerusalem, that he passed through the midst of Samaria and Galilee.

And as he entered into a certain village, there met him ten men that were lepers, which stood afar off:

And they lifted up their voices, and said, Jesus, Master, have mercy on us.

And when he saw them, he said unto them, **Go** shew yourselves unto the priests. And it came to pass, that, as they went, they were cleansed.

And one of them, when he saw that he was healed, turned back, and with a loud voice glorified **God,**

And fell down on his face at his feet, giving him thanks: and he was a Samaritan.

And Jesus answering said, Were there not ten cleansed? but where are the nine?

Only one in ten returned to give thanks in Christ's day. Today's average would not be much better. Surely, each of us can do his or her part to raise this average.

✓   ✓   ✓

One of my neighbors suffered the loss of a child. The mortician who was called in went so far out of his way in the thoughtful things he did that, upon receiving his bill, my neighbor and his wife called on him to thank him for his many kindnesses, and to ask if he felt sure he had charged enough to cover all his time and trouble.

The mortician assured them that the bill was adequate. He told them that as a young man he had aspired to be a doctor, but had lacked the money for the years of necessary education.

"So I decided on my present profession, and made up my mind to put myself as wholeheartedly into my service as though I were a great physician, motivated by a genuine love for humanity," he explained. "This has been my guiding philosophy for more than twenty years, yet you good people are the first ones ever to call on me and thank me. Need I tell you that you have paid your bill doubly by your kindness?"

I like to think of "Thank you" as a tiny gift-token which can be used to make the giving of anything a *two-way* transaction, enjoyable to the original giver and the thanks-giver.

Also, I try to remember that money alone cannot pay for especially cheerful or efficient service, or for a particularly fine job of work. The person who serves us superlatively gives us something of himself, over and above the actual requirements of his job or profession. If we would square the account, we must in return give something of ourselves.

✦ ✦ ✦

None of us is ever too busy to pay his way. It takes only a few seconds to say a heart-warming "Thank you." Probably no American of modern times lived a more hurried or hectic life than Theodore Roosevelt. Yet even on political campaign trips, when in the hustle and bustle he might have been excused from thinking of other people, it was his custom as he left his private train to stop and thank the engineer and fireman for a safe and comfortable trip. It took but a fraction of a minute of his time, but he had two more friends for the rest of his life.

"Good politics," you may say. But good living too—for after all, isn't having friends the basis of happy living, as well as of successful politics?

Nor have I found any situation in which thanks cannot be given. You can thank even total strangers with a nod of the head, a gesture of the hand in traffic, a grateful glance in jostling street crowds, a smile in swaying subway trains, a nod in the quiet of a church service. Anywhere at all, if your heart is saying "Thank you."

Isn't it time all of us *did* something about the inexcusable one-in-ten average of those who bother to return to give thanks? Wouldn't you like to be one of a million volunteers to set out in serious fashion to better this average?

60

Chapter 18

Little Sparks of Appreciation

Life would be much more exciting if each of us left a trail of "little sparks of appreciation" along our way.

Your wife makes a tasty omelette. Do you tell her how good it is? She may tire of making omelettes, but she will never tire of sincere compliments. What is more, she will enjoy making the next omelette.

One of your children gets a good mark on an examination. Do you show your appreciation by sitting down with the youngster and going over the paper, expressing your pleasure over each right answer? Nothing pleases children more than this kind of parental interest and approval.

You enjoy your dinner in a restaurant. Do you tell the waiter so? He gets terribly tired of serving food all day to people who seem to get no special pleasure out of their meals. A word of appreciation will add a touch of dignity to his job.

A salesgirl shows you unusual courtesy, or is particularly patient in serving you. Do you mention it appreciatively? Her feet probably hurt, and her spirit may be low. Certainly she is weary of waiting on people who treat her as part of the store's equipment.

Your pastor preaches a particularly fine sermon. Do you take a minute to go up to him after the service and express your enjoyment? Every minister, lecturer, and public speaker knows the discouragement of pouring himself out to an audience, and not receiving a single appreciative comment. It is not necessary even to wait until afterward to make your appreciation felt. The deadpan expression of audiences is the despair of public speakers. A single appreciative face stands out and is a source of inspiration.

In the early days of radio when performers worked in silent studios, many of them found it impossible to give good performances. Studio audiences were introduced—and stage managed—to supply the appreciation which is essential even to professional entertainers.

✓ ✓ ✓

What applies to professionals applies doubly to workers in offices, stores, factories, laboratories, or studios. In our working relations we should try to remember that the girl at the next counter, the man at the next bench or machine, the person at the adjoining desk or in the next office, is a human being first of all, and after that a salesperson, machinist, cost accountant, or department head. And all human beings hunger for appreciation.

Leaving a friendly trail of little sparks of appreciation is largely a matter of cultivating the habit of reflecting your happiness by expressing it to the people around you. It will prove a heart-warming habit—for them and for you.

Chapter 19

A Reader Makes a Discovery

A letter from a reader says, "Before I read your book I always thought you had to join an organization to help people. Now I know you can do simple things all by yourself that will make people happy."

This is an important discovery. Organizations are wonderful, and of course they must carry much of the load of helping people, particularly the disadvantaged. They deserve our full support.

But each of us can be a one-man or one-woman organization to give of ourselves in little personal ways that no organization can possibly match. And this to the advantaged and disadvantaged alike. Such personal giving often touches people's lives in peculiarly helpful ways.

✓ ✓ ✓

Carrying on the activities of any organization usually involves a considerable annual outlay of money. Even most volunteer organizations require a paid director, and often at least a small staff. Many of them have to rent office space, and they require telephone service, stationery, and usually printed literature. Their postage bill, also, can be a considerable item.

In short, the most efficient organization has to be staffed and equipped before it can start its giving. Whereas you and I have only to make up our mind to obey our little giving-impulses and we are in business!

⁊   ⁊   ⁊

This does not relieve us of any responsibilities we may presently be carrying in some organization that is serving people's needs. Rather, it suggests that we can add our own personal giving-away to our organization work. If, in all our activities and contacts as representatives of the organization, we will give an extra bit of human warmth—in terms of interest, sympathy, understanding, helpfulness—we will be giving with *double empathy*: empathy for the organization and empathy for ourselves personally.

Chapter 20

Appreciation-in-Depth

When some people express their appreciation it seems to have a special quality which I have come to think of as *depth*.

At first I thought depth was a matter of sincerity or warmth. But the more I studied the most successful appreciators, the surer I was that neither of these qualities, nor both of them together, fully explained *depth*.

And then, one day, I saw clearly what it was: their appreciation was always *specific*.

They did not say merely, "I enjoyed your concert." They said, "I enjoyed every number on your program, but *particularly* the Chopin group."

They did not say merely, "I liked your book ever so much." They said, "Your book was so exciting that I couldn't lay it down until I'd finished it, well after midnight."

They did not say merely, "This pie is delicious." They said, "This is a delicious pie—the crust is so flaky."

They did not say merely, "Thank you for the flowers you sent me." They said, "The lovely flowers you sent me blended in so perfectly with my table decorations that several of my guests commented on it."

While general statements of pleasure or appreciation may

cover the etiquette of the situation, they fall far short of the opportunity to give pleasure. They are lacking in depth of thought; they reveal no discrimination.

I had always thought my expressions of appreciation adequate until I made this discovery. Then I realized how shallow they had been, and how unsatisfying to the recipients.

✓ ✓ ✓

You may be a natural appreciator-in-depth. If you are not, I promise that if you begin to seek out the specific you will not only find that your appreciation is received with greater pleasure; you will get greater enjoyment yourself from the things you are appreciating, for you will be exercising greater discrimination in analyzing and evaluating them.

After all, if we appreciate something, it is usually for a specific reason. If we train ourselves to analyze the reason, we will have the basis for appreciation-in-depth.

✓ ✓ ✓

Still another virtue of being specific is illustrated by the experience of a now-famous woman writer. One morning she received a letter from a stranger telling her how much she had enjoyed the writer's story in a current magazine. The letter went on to tell just what parts of the story had proved especially interesting.

This letter happened to arrive in the same mail which brought back one of the writer's stories from another magazine with a rejection slip. As balm to her depressed spirits, a few hours later she got out the note of appreciation and reread it. Suddenly she saw that the things singled out for favorable comment in her published story were missing in the one that had been rejected. She sat right down and rewrote the story, and had the pleasure, a few weeks later, of selling it—to the very magazine which had originally returned it.

The *specific* gives people something to work on.

✔   ✔   ✔

But mark this: Appreciation must be sincere to be acceptable. We usually know when something we do merits approval or compliment, and we are suspicious of people who praise us undeservedly. A specific comment shows the recipient that we have given thought to what we say, but by the same token it is the more transparent if not honest.

Chapter 21

Are You a "Noticer"?

A seriously neglected aspect of the art of appreciation is the habit of *noticing*.

All of us put much thought into selecting our clothes, laying out and caring for our gardens, decorating our homes and adding to their furnishings, training our children, planning menus for our meals, polishing our cars, and all the other day-to-day activities of living. One of the minor disappointments of life is that our family, friends, and neighbors are prone to take for granted all our thought and pains; they so seldom seem to *notice*.

When someone does notice, and speaks admiringly of our efforts, it pleases us inordinately. And is that not a fine gift—inordinate pleasure?

✦ ✦ ✦

Merchants and businessmen give much thought to the products and services they offer the public. They plan with great care their advertising, their window displays, their packages, their catalogs and sales literature, the layout of their offices, the lighting and sanitation of their factories. It is disappointing to them that ninety-eight people out of a hundred seemingly fail to notice what they have done, let alone speak any word of appreciaton.

In taking for granted all of this care and thought, you and I are shortchanging the merchants and businessmen who serve us—and ourselves as well.

✔   ✔   ✔

Years ago, when I was virtually commuting between New York and Chicago on the Twentieth Century Limited, as I slipped into my berth one night, I noticed that it was made up with soft rose-colored blankets not unlike those on my bed at home.

"This indeed deserves an expression of appreciation," I told myself. Upon my return home I wrote a note to the president of the Pullman Company in which I said:

I want to register my enthusiastic appreciation for the new soft blankets you are now using in your sleeping cars. They are a most welcome change from the heavy boardlike blankets that have been used on Pullman berths all these years.

Since I travel about a week each month, you can appreciate that I am delighted to have these more homelike blankets to spread over me when I go to bed on the train.

A few days later I received a friendly letter from the Pullman president thanking me earnestly for my note, and going on with three paragraphs of interesting facts about "Pullman housekeeping." It was a heart-warming exchange of correspondence.

✔   ✔   ✔

If you cultivate the habit of noticing—and speaking of— all sorts of little things, you soon begin to earn an unexpected double dividend on your giving: You become more *alert* to the life that is going on around you. You seem somehow to *savor* it more, to enjoy its spirit and color and variety. Not only that; you get a reputation for being a person of discrimination—which you actually become because you are constantly exercising your powers of observation and appreciation.

A good noticer is indeed a great pleasure-giver.

Chapter 22

Experiments in Interest-Giving

In my hobby of collecting practically costless ways of giving, I tried an experiment one evening.

My wife and I were invited to dinner at the home of a man whose hobby is collecting postage stamps. I had always been bored with stamp collections, and I rather dreaded it when my host said after dinner, "Would you be interested in seeing my stamp collection?"

Then this thought flashed into my mind, "Well, I've got to see it anyway. Why not try giving him the pleasure of having a really *interested* listener?"

"I would," I said, and I really meant it, for I was going to practice my own hobby while he indulged his.

So, instead of merely paying polite attention, while devoutly hoping our hostess would come to the rescue by suggesting a game of bridge, I got into the spirit of his hobby. It did not take him long to realize, from the look in my eyes and the questions I asked, that I was genuinely interested. Drawing on his broad knowledge of stamps and their history and geography, he held me fascinated for more than an hour. I was not half ready to have him stop when his wife did suggest bridge.

I had given my friend the pleasure of showing his stamp collection, and in return he had given me one of the most enjoyable hours I had spent in many months.

That night I came to the conclusion that the reason the world often seems dull and unexciting is because we are so wrapped up in our own narrow interests and prejudices that we resist it when other people try to take us into their lives. Whereas, if we would give them our interest, they would open up realms which would prove fascinating to us.

ツ ツ ツ

To realize what an acceptable gift we bestow when we give our close attention and interest to other people's hobbies and experiences, we have only to recall what pleasure we get when we encounter a good listener who seems genuinely interested in our travels, our garden, our library; or in being shown our stamps or guns or butterflies, or whatever it is we collect. He makes us relive our experiences enjoyably. We warm up to him and come to look upon him as a true friend.

We may be sure that others will feel the same toward us if we enter their worlds wholeheartedly, instead of merely stepping politely across the threshold, with one eye on the door, ready to back out the minute we decently can.

ツ ツ ツ

After the episode of the stamp collection, I tried many experiments in interest-giving. One of the earliest was in my days of train travel. One night, from Chicago to Buffalo, I sat in the Pullman smoking room reading a novel. The only other occupant was a man who sat looking out the window into the night, rather glumly it seemed to me.

"I wonder," I said to myself, "If this man may not be more interesting than the novel I am reading."

I shut the book. "You don't look as though you are enjoying this trip," I said.

"No," he said, scarcely glancing at me. "I get fed up with travel." I thought that was the end of it, that he had slammed the door in my face. But in a few seconds he said, "I'm a traveling engineer."

"What might a traveling engineer be?" I asked.

"A sort of trouble shooter," he explained. "They send me out in the cab when the engineer on a run can't make the time called for on the schedule. Or when they're working out the running time for a new train. I'm rolling practically all the time."

"I'm very much interested," I said. "Tell me more."

He squared around so he was facing me, with one leg up on the leather cushion, and for two hours related his experiences. He told me of wrecks he had been in, and of the unbelievable speeds he had traveled on test runs of locomotives. He was bound for New York where he was scheduled to test, with empty Pullmans, the new articulated roller-bearing Twentieth Century Limited, in anticipation of reducing its running time between New York and Chicago from eighteen to sixteen hours.

When we parted at midnight his face was aglow with pleasure—and so was mine. We had both had a thoroughly enjoyable evening. I had learned many interesting things about railroading, and I have a hunch he enjoyed his work more from that night on. When we give a fellowman a fresh appreciation of the interest and importance of his job, are we not doing him a fine service?

I did not finish the novel I was reading. Only the best novels are as interesting as the experience and hobbies of the people around us, if we would take the trouble to give them *our* interest.

Chapter 23

I Get a Jolt in the Subway

Much more recently, I was riding from Brooklyn Bridge to Grand Central in a jammed New York subway express one evening in the rush hour, swaying dangerously with the mass of my fellow standees in spite of having a strap to clutch.

"New York is an inhuman city, David," I told myself as another installment of humanity crowded into the train at the Fourteenth Street stop.

A minute later we were zinging along toward Grand Central when, suddenly, the emergency brakes grabbed. If we hadn't been so tightly packed in, all of us would have been thrown to the floor. As it was, my feet were stepped on, one of my arms was twisted, and someone's elbow jabbed into my back so hard that I thought my spine would crack.

In my irritation I turned my head to make an ungracious remark to the owner of the elbow. He was a tall man with a long, thin, rather funereal face. But there was a disarming twinkle in his eyes. As I started to speak he murmured, "Terribly sorry, my friend." Then, in a voice loud enough to be heard halfway down the car, he announced, "Unscheduled stop. All change for Good Nature."

There was a spontaneous burst of laughter, then a banter

of witty wisecracks such as only a sophisticated New York crowd can think up in seconds. In no time there was almost a carnival spirit at our end of that subway car!

"You are Mr. Good Nature himself," I said to my friend of the sharp elbow, thoroughly ashamed of my own lack of good nature. "New York needs *thousands* of you."

"It's a great city—if you keep your good nature in good working order. Otherwise . . ." The car swayed so that I couldn't hear the rest. Anyway, I was delivering a lecture to myself. "You of all people, David," I chided myself, "neglecting to practice your hobby right here in the City of New York. Have you lost your faith? Or is it your imagination?"

As I climbed the steep stairs at Grand Central to catch my suburban train, it came to me in a sudden flash: My friend of the sharp elbow had glimpsed the New York that *might be* . . . Good natured . . . Friendly . . . Human.

But it wasn't until I was taking a walk after supper that I began to get the picture of what a really human city New York might be. I reminded myself that New York was not City Hall, or the skyscrapers, or the Brooklyn Bridge, or Greenwich Village, or Grand Central, or Fifth Avenue, or Harlem, or Central Park, or the East River, or the Battery. *"New York is its PEOPLE—starting with each of its citizens as individuals,"* I told myself . . . *"And so is every other city, big or little."*

✦   ✦   ✦

Then I reminded myself that the reason people crowd into a big city to live is because there are already so many people in the city that it will support theaters, concerts, lectures, first-run movies, museums, libraries, art galleries, fine hotels and restaurants, shops of every description, banks and broker-age houses, churches of every denomination, wonderful hospitals with staffs of celebrated specialists, all manner of educational opportunities. In short, the makings for truly rewarding living for all the members of the family.

The trouble is, when we move to a big city from a small city or town or village, we forget to pack in the van that moves our furniture, or in our personal luggage, the most precious ingredients of life in a small place—humanness. The cheerful "good mornings," the friendliness, the neighborly interest, the courtesy.

Instead, arriving in the impersonal city, we promptly become just one more thoughtlessly impersonal citizen.

"Shame on us—all of us!" I exclaimed aloud.

✓ ✓ ✓

I am not a regular commuter, but I do go to the city quite often. I now realized that, on arriving in the city I had—quite unconsciously—been failing to look for the scores of little ways one can give, even to total strangers, in a crowded city. It was as though I had been excusing myself with the alibi, "You can't possibly humanize a big city like New York."

But my experience in the subway that afternoon had proved to me that *a big city can be humanized.* My friend of the sharp elbow had proved it!

On my next trip to New York I took my hobby with me in good working order.

It was noon when I arrived at Grand Central. I decided to go to a restaurant near the station for lunch before tackling my afternoon schedule.

The service was terribly slow. I was starting to drum impatiently on the table top when the waitress came to take my order. I noticed she was limping. "Time to do a bit of humanizing, David," I told myself.

"I'll bet your feet hurt you today," I said with a friendly smile.

She looked startled, then smiled back. "Not my feet. My back. The bus boy for my station didn't show up today. Carrying the heavy trays is almost getting me down. And it sure has slowed me *up*," she added with a grin.

"I'll order a light lunch," I said jokingly, "so it won't be too heavy to carry." We both grinned.

For dessert I had ordered fresh strawberries. As she placed a heaping dish of berries in front of me she leaned down and whispered, "Thanks for the lift, mister. The trays are lighter now."

Obeying an impulse had made New York just a tiny mite more human for both of us. And my lunch had tasted better.

✦ ✦ ✦

Walking to my next appointment, on one of the side streets in the fifties, I noticed a young woman tortuously maneuvering her long station wagon out of a tight space parallel to the curb. She had backed in and filled as much space as she possibly could and was obviously fearful that she would now snag the fender of the brand new Cadillac in front of her. She looked utterly helpless.

I could see that she would just barely clear. Instead of telling myself that her predicament was not my funeral, as all the other passersby were doing, I stopped and called to her; "Go ahead—*very* slowly." I watched until she was in the clear, then waved her on her way with a friendly smile.

"Oh, *thank* you," she called. Then, impulsively, she blew me a gay little kiss!

"New York isn't such a bad city!" I told myself with a grin. And I'm sure she was thinking the same.

✓ ✓ ✓

A couple of hours later I discovered that I wasn't the city's only giver-away. As I was walking down Madison Avenue a man just ahead of me stooped and picked up a newspaper which someone had thoughtlessly discarded in the middle of the sidewalk, and he dropped it into the wire trash receptacle at the corner.

"Good work, neighbor," I said as I came abreast of him. And then I bethought myself of something I had read the night before. "Last night," I told him, "I was reading James Michener's *Iberia*. He tells of a sign in the gardens of a Spanish city which reads, 'These gardens are for all and are to be cared for by all.'"

"Wonderful!" he exclaimed. "If the people of New York would only adopt *that* attitude, what a fine, clean city we would have!"

"The New York that might be," said I. He nodded and we went our separate ways, leaving a little spot of human warmth on a Madison Avenue corner.

✓ ✓ ✓

That evening I was staying in town to finish a job at the office before taking a taxi to La Guardia Airport for a night flight to the West.

As I signed myself out at nine o'clock in the night watchman's book in the drafty lobby, it flashed to me that his was a very cold and lonely job. How could I cheer his evening?

"Have you heard the Ike and Mike story?" I asked, recalling a cute story I had heard recently. And I told him the story, which has a comical surprise ending.

"That's a *good* one, Mr. Dunn! Good night and *thank* you."

There was a warmth in his voice that warmed my own heart all the dreary way to La Guardia.

Ever since I have been having a ball, giving away little 25¢ portions of myself to humanize this great big, lonely city.

I've been at it long enough to see clearly that if we citizens allow ourselves to be sour, selfish, unfriendly, discourteous, antagonistic—and worst of all, fatalistic—there is no hope for our cities. BUT, if we make up our minds to be cheerful, friendly, smiling, courteous, sympathetic, helpful, and hopeful at every opportunity, before we know it we'll be living in our city-that-might-be.

✓   ✓   ✓

Let's make no mistake about it, the city officials, the police force, the city's many institutions, its clubs, churches, schools, theaters, hotels, and newspapers can't do the *humanizing* necessary to make our cities livable. They can help, of course, but it is *we ordinary citizens*—all of us together—who are creating the spirit of our city, every day, whether it be New York, Omaha, Seattle, Dallas, Boston, New Orleans, Portland. And what is true of every big city is true also of every smaller city.

The hard, unforgivable fact is that every twenty-four hours we city people are thoughtlessly throwing away literally *millions* of opportunities to do friendly courteous, kindly, helpful, surprising little things that would make ours a wonderfully human city.

I shall never forget the citizen of Cairo, Egypt, who walked two blocks with me, a stranger, one Sunday morning a few years ago to make sure I found the address I showed him on a slip of paper. In spite of all the criticism of the Egyptians, that Sunday-morning courtesy has left me with a memory of Cairo as a friendly city.

✓ ✓ ✓

No matter what your age, sex, race, religion, education, occupation or politics, you can do your 25¢ worth—a dozen or more times every day—to humanize your city. Starting at your doorstep in the morning. (How much more *lively* our "good mornings" could be!) On the sidewalk. (A smiling face.) Driving in traffic. (What a wealth of opportunities to show consideration here!) Likewise in taxis or buses, or the subway. (As so dramatically demonstrated.) In your work place. (A priceless opportunity to create a happy work-spirit!) Shopping in a supermarket or department store. In restaurants, hotel lobbies, elevators. In your church, school, club, apartment house. (Particularly in your apartment house!)

And always smiling at the children you pass. (Children should grow up in a smiling city!)

Looking for things to praise or compliment. Speaking well of your neighbors, whenever you possibly can. Always adding a smile to your greetings, your "thank you's."

As for the people right around you, trying to find *something* to like about everybody you meet or deal with. People just can't resist being liked! They have to start liking you back!

We are all so very human. We sorely need to be understood, appreciated, cheered, thanked, complimented, encouraged.

Another important way you can do your 25¢ worth of city humanizing: Start talking with the people you meet about the things you *like* about the city, and lay off the thoughtless knocking of the things we don't like. (This often proves surprisingly contagious, I find.)

Of course, you will be a bit self-conscious when you first start giving yourself to your city. And occasionally you will be misunderstood, perhaps even rudely rebuffed. What of it? You will soon learn how to give yourself easily and acceptably. As a matter of fact, what every city needs, first and foremost, is to be *thawed out*. When enough of us start giving ourselves, the thawing-out process will start—and suspicion and rebuffing will go out of fashion!

✓ ✓ ✓

Occasionally, when I am tired or out of sorts, or when I stand off and look at my big, crowded, impersonal city, it seems to be too much trouble to give myself, even in little ways. I have a homemade slogan that I repeat to myself at such times: *"I'll do it for a friendlier New York."*

The effect of repeating this simple resolve is magical! It lifts a little giving-away impulse out of its littleness and makes it part of a big and important crusade of making the city *livable*.

New York hasn't any patent on this magical resolve. It can read, "I'll do it for a friendlier —————." Just fill in the name of your own city and you will be in business as a city-humanizer!

Chapter 24

A Winter Morning News Broadcast

By a curious coincidence, a few mornings after I wrote the preceding chapter, when I turned on the seven o'clock news broadcast I listened to the following story:

The afternoon before the Staten Island Ferry had been making one of its regular trips to the Battery at the tip of Manhattan. The passengers were interested only in themselves, "just as New Yorkers always are—sophisticated and impersonal."

Suddenly there was a scream: "Somebody's overboard." This jolted the self-centered passengers enough to send them to the rail. Looking down they could see the head of a woman in the water. A life preserver had been thrown to her but she made no move toward it.

The Captain, realizing that she was suffering shock from her icy plunge, called for a volunteer to plunge in and rescue her. The passengers looked at one another but no one moved.

Suddenly a young man in the crowd pulled off his coat and shoes, handed his camera to a bystander, grabbed a life jacket, and jumped into the water and rescued the woman.

At the hospital she was found to be in deep shock and, at the time of the broadcast; could not tell her story, or even be identified.

As for the young man, he was cold and soaked to the skin, but otherwise seemed none the worse for the experience. All that could be found out about him, before he slipped quietly away with his camera, was that he was from a small town in Wisconsin, and had been in New York just twenty hours. As someone expressed it, "Not long enough to smother the natural friendliness and helpfulness of a small town, and turn him into an impersonal and uncaring big-city-ite."

*　*　*

None of us is likely to be called upon to plunge heroically into New York harbor on a winter morning to rescue a stranger. But not one of us need settle for being "an impersonal and uncaring big-city-ite," no matter what big city we happen to live in.

It may seem like we are taking a cold plunge into the icy waters of indifference and suspicion when we start a personal program of doing our modest part in humanizing our city. But we'll soon discover that the water isn't nearly as cold as we expected it to be. And first thing we know, we'll find our city is a much friendlier place than we realized.

The friendliness is there in every city, just waiting to be released!

Chapter 25

The Poverty of the Wealthy and the Loneliness of the Great

Money and fame can represent a curious form of poverty —the poverty of the human spirit when left to itself. Neither money nor fame would be of the slightest value to an individual if he were stranded on an uninhabited island in a remote spot in the ocean, or in the middle of a great desert.

Money and fame are only wealth in relation to *people*. Yet, oddly enough, they tend to insulate their owners from their fellow human beings.

The very wealthy man soon discovers that so many of those around him are scheming to get some of his money, either for themselves or for some pet cause, that he begins to wonder if he has any true friends interested in him for himself. The suspicion gives him a curious sense of loneliness.

He tries to spend his money to buy the satisfactions of the spirit, but finds that it will purchase few. This is because satisfactions of the spirit do not come from material possessions or from costly living, but from friendly human experiences. And these have to be *given;* seldom can they be *bought*.

One afternoon I drove around a Florida resort in a Ford runabout with a very wealthy man. Someone with little money but a sound knowledge of human nature had given him an inexpensive little gadget that made a saucy birdcall when he pulled a string. Every time he did this the pedestrians in our path would scatter. But the bird had such a funny warble, and my millionaire friend wore such a happy grin, that all along the street people turned to laugh and wave to us. We laughed and waved back. We were all friends.

The magic of the gadget was that it broke down the barrier between this man's millions and the world of plain people.

✓ ✓ ✓

The great—whether they be opera stars or movie queens, famous authors or television artists, explorers or scientists— often suffer keenly from the insulation of their greatness. They may appear to be utterly self-sufficient, and some of them put on a show of being cynically indifferent to their fan mail. But they are not; deep down inside most of them love it! The publicity manufactured to build them up does not warm their hearts. What they crave is the spontaneous, human, affectionate appreciation of the people they are trying to please.

None of us can live within ourselves; we must, if we are to be truly happy, have a sense that the world likes us and values what we can do, or appreciates what we have made of ourselves.

August corporation presidents, bankers, labor leaders, lawyers, scientists, college presidents—all prize unsolicited expressions of approval and appreciation from members of the public. I have known the head of a famous airline to carry in his pocket for weeks a letter from a humble woman passenger commending one of his policies, which he showed to friends and associates with almost childish pleasure.

In the realm of politics we are all too ready to criticize our elected representatives and our civil servants when what they do displeases us, but we seldom think to commend them for actions which we approve.

When we write a note of appreciation or commendation to any man or woman in the public eye, we should not expect a reply. Many of these people do not have a secretary; and many of those who do have are so busy that they cannot possibly dictate personal acknowledgments of all the letters they receive. But they appreciate hearing from the public just the same.

And how can you know that your word of appreciation or commendation will not strengthen or encourage some great person at a critical hour in his or her life?

I think often of the loneliness of Abraham Lincoln as he left the Gettysburg battlefield after his address. We think today that Lincoln must have realized that this Gettysburg address would live in men's hearts; but how could he possibly have known this? After the long, flowery speech of Edward Everett, the orator of the day, which drew thunderous applause from the crowd, his simple speech was received in silence. He could not know that his hearers were so moved by his message that applause would have seemed sacrilege. He could not foresee that his words would one day be cast in imperishable bronze, and be taught every school child in the land. He could not know—because no one told him.

If only some mother had timidly plucked his sleeve as he made his way through the crowd back to the train, and said, "Mr. Lincoln, I have given a son in this war, but your words have healed the ache in my heart."

It takes bigness of spirit to praise the great and the successful, instead of envying them.

George Matthew Adams wrote: "He who praises another enriches himself far more than he does the one praised. To praise is an investment in happiness . . . The poorest human being has something to give that the richest could not buy."

Chapter 26

On Being Socially Useful

Today's college generation is undergoing a very sober time of turmoil and adjustment. Youth promises to be impatient, not only with the educational processes, but with the aims of education, particularly objecting to the emphasis that has been placed on educating for "success" and "getting ahead."

It might be characterized as a generation putting more emphasis on *giving* than *getting*. Or at least of working out a more equitable balance between getting and giving. Which is greatly to its credit.

The problem is to work out the way to do this.

✶   ✶   ✶

Brought up in an affluent generation, this rather idealistic generation naturally takes the material things of life for granted—comfortable homes, the clothes they need, plenty of food, education, automobiles, TV and radio, travel, etc., etc. Their parents and grandparents could not take these things for granted; they had to work and save and plan continually to arrive at so comfortable a standard of living for themselves and their children. And the older ones lived through the Great Depression, which caused them to try to accumulate sufficient money and material things to protect themselves and their children.

Whether or not these children are critical of what they consider the materialistic attitude of their parents is beside the point. The fact is, the young people who are coming out of our colleges are contributing a valuable new concept to our times: the concept of being *socially useful;* of not just making a *living,* but making a *life*.

✦   ✦   ✦

In the matter of being socially useful, comparatively few of us can hold influential positions in government as elected or appointed state, city, or town officials. But all of us can be socially useful in our community affairs, as members and workers in local organizations, and in church, educational, lodge, and club activities. Also in our business or professional organizations, on a broader scale.

Importantly, every one of us, regardless of age, color, or economic status, can make ourselves socially useful by giving bits of ourselves daily to those around us, in little ways that will make life more livable in our community. And we should never forget that our nation—and the world—is merely a multiplication of local communities.

I am constantly surprised at the imaginative ways people are finding to give themselves away usefully to their neighbors, as described in the letters I receive. And by people who frankly admit they didn't know they had it in them to do such giving. They feel that they are *discovering* themselves—as of course they are. Even more broadly, they are discovering life and the opportunities it offers for being of service to their fellow humans.

Perhaps out of the agitation going on in our colleges the young generation is making a significant contribution to the times by turning the spotlight on the concept of every citizen being socially useful.

Social usefulness would be a marvelous giving-away hobby for any young man or woman to adopt—for life!

Chapter 27

The Finest Heart Tonic in the World

Not long after I became interested in giving-away as a hobby, I made a second important discovery. I had heard other men tell about how, at times when they were low in spirit or worried about something, they would sneak out for a golf lesson, or spend an evening going over their fishing gear or fussing with their collection of old firearms, and their spirit would rise. Well, I discovered that if I turned to my new hobby I got the same lift. The reason was, of course, that it took me out of myself.

When you are feeling sorry for yourself, it requires a little more conscious effort to start looking around for some way to give yourself away than it does when you are feeling gay and generous. But it works like magic!

Suppose you wake up grumpy, or actually belligerent—as who doesn't once in a while? You are quite sure that nothing or nobody can make you feel cheerful. You are just in for a low day, and that's that.

Then is the time of all times to begin looking for some way to give yourself, not in order to be goody-goody, but for the completely practical purpose of jockeying yourself into a position where you can't help being happy.

I remember sitting at breakfast early one morning, years ago, at a lunch counter near the South Station in Boston. Having arrived on the sleeper from New York, and been routed out before seven o'clock after a poor night's sleep, I was feeling very sorry for David Dunn.

"What you have to accomplish in Boston today is too important to risk failure just because you feel grumpy," I told myself sternly. "You'd better start giving-away . . . But how can you give-away sitting on a stool in a row of other grumpy night travelers before seven o'clock in the morning?" I argued with myself.

And then I thought of the salt and pepper! I recalled reading of some woman who said she was sure her husband loved her dearly—but he *never* thought to pass her the salt and pepper. I had noticed ever since how important salt and pepper often are to our enjoyment of meals, and how seldom anyone takes the trouble to pass them to us.

I glanced up and down the counter. The only salt and pepper shakers in sight were directly in front of *me*. I had already seasoned my fried eggs, with no thought of my fellow breakfasters. Now, picking up the shakers, I offered them to the man on my right.

"Perhaps you—and some of the other people down the line—can use these," I said.

He thanked me, seasoned his eggs, and passed the shakers on. Every person at the counter used them.

That broke the ice. I got into conversation with my neighbor, and the man next to him joined in. Before I knew it everyone at the counter was talking, and presently we were all laughing and joking, eating breakfasts seasoned with salt, pepper, and good humor. And I had supplied the seasoning!

93

By the time I had finished my breakfast I was feeling positively cheerful. My mission in Boston that day worked out better than I had thought possible.

✓   ✓   ✓

Walking downtown on an errand one morning, for some silly reason I was feeling out of sorts with the world. "Why not try giving?" I asked myself. I looked around for someone to give to. The only prospect in sight was a little girl sitting on the doorstep of the house I was passing. She appeared about as forlorn as I felt.

"That's a *very* pretty red dress you are wearing, young lady," I said.

"Oh, thank you," she said, looking down at her dress, her face lighting up at this surprising comment from a stranger— and a man, at that.

Her face was still alight when I passed her house half an hour later on my way home. "Hello, Man!" she hailed me. I had a new friend. And my little gift of a compliment had lifted both of us out of the dumps.

✓   ✓   ✓

I can claim no scientific basis for the point I now make, but I believe it to be sound: Giving-away is not only good for the spirit; it is also a beneficial heart stimulant.

It is my conviction that health is to no small extent conditioned, perhaps even controlled, by the circulation of the blood. That important little circulatory organ located in the left side of the chest is, I believe, influenced to a greater degree than we perhaps realize by that other "heart" which is described in the dictionary as "the seat of the affections; the emotional nature."

When your emotional nature is stirred by something you do, is it not probable that your heart is actually stimulated, so that it quickens the circulation of your blood and makes you feel alive and full of health?

I know that the little surges of happiness I get out of giving-away suffuse me with a momentary sense of glowing health. I have come to believe that my hobby of giving-away, with the flush of pleasure it brings, is the finest heart tonic in the world!

Chapter 28

Giving-Away by Giving-Up

Seemingly a hobbyist becomes also a collector. At least I have. I keep collecting new ways to practice my hobby. Some of them come from the letters I have received from readers of this book, who have told me interesting ways they have worked out for giving themselves away. Others I stumble upon as I bump along through life. (And isn't that what most of us are doing these difficult days?)

For example, it struck me one day that, along with most everybody else, in talking with people, in my reading, and in watching TV, I had fallen into the habit of reacting first to the things I *disagreed* with, in what was being said.

At a time when there is so much disagreement, between generations, between races, between nations, and between everyday people of opposing points of view on so many subjects, our natural tendency is to look first at our disagreements. In doing this we rudely slam the door against each other. And at a time when what the world needs most is thinking and working *together*.

So I started an experiment in a new kind of giving. In my contacts with people, young or old, friends or mere acquaintances, with whom I find myself in disagreement, I probe conversationally until I find something on which I believe we could agree. And I let him (or her) know that I do agree, and I am as enthusiastic as I can honestly be.

It may be about a front-page news event, a local problem, a certain person known to both of us, a TV program. In short, about anything at all that might serve to dovetail our minds about *something*. Soon enough we may encounter something about the news event, the local problem, the certain person, or the TV program that I may have suspected we would not agree about. But first agreeing about something helps to create a climate of agreeability and ease which makes for friendly discussion.

This might be said to be *giving-away* by *giving-up*—for the time being at least—the all-too-human right to start out right away to disagree.

✦ ✦ ✦

At first I was a bit clumsy and self-conscious about giving-up. And once in a while a particularly antagonistic person would deliberately repulse my attempt to find a point of agreement.

But in a very short time I found myself intrigued by the challenge of finding a point of agreement to start with. My new form of giving had become a series of mini-adventures in human nature. And I have found that disagreeing, even vehemently, on other points is much less painful if we have agreed on *something* at the start.

I can't help wondering what miracles it would work, in these unkindly times, if in our community life, our local and national political life, and our international relations, all of us—young and old, black and white, individuals and nations—would make a practice of *first* looking, honestly and constructively, for at least some point of possible agreement. Instead of starting personal conversations, meetings, conferences, and congresses with points of difference, or automatically jumping into print or radio or TV with opening statements of disagreement, if only we would first look for something on which we can agree.

We need not abandon our ideas or ideals. And certainly we should not violate our convictions. But, as individuals, races, and nations, we can at least approach each other with courtesy and in a spirit of fairness. I am convinced that we will often come nearer to eventual agreement on controversial ideas and issues if we *start* with agreement on *something*.

$$\checkmark \quad \checkmark \quad \checkmark$$

Obviously, we private citizens can have no direct influence in national or world affairs, but the longer I practice my hobby of giving myself away, the more impressed I am with the fact that a better, more livable world must start with *us*.

Who can say that the spirit of our giving—with its courtesy, reasonableness, and empathy—may not spread in circling ripples until it begins to set a kindlier and more common-sense pattern of human relations?

Truly, this would be a big return on a very small investment in giving-up!

Chapter 29

Giving Yourself to a Group

One of my friends used to be painfully self-conscious in a group. He dreaded to enter a roomful of people. One day he made the interesting discovery that he could overcome this diffidence by, as he expresses it, "giving myself to the group."

This is his technique: Whenever he steps into a room where there are several persons, he glances around to see if there is not something he can do to make someone in the room happier or more comfortable.

For instance, it may be that the sun is shining in someone's eyes. Or there may be no ash tray near someone who is smoking. Or it may be evident that moving a floor lamp will throw a better light over the shoulder of a person who is reading or playing a game. Or perhaps a cocktail glass has been left on the edge of a table where it is sure to be knocked off. Or a lighted cigarette is poised precariously on the rim of an ash tray, ready to fall and burn the table cover. Or he may notice that a chair has been left in a position where people are likely to bump into it.

This man does not make the mistake of rushing to do something about any of these situations. He watches his opportunity quietly to lower the shade a little. He looks around for an unused ash tray and places it beside the smoker, without comment. He quietly moves the floor lamp the necessary inches to throw a better light. He moves the cocktail glass to a safe place. He shifts the chair to make a clear passage. All of these little services he performs unobtrusively as he talks with people.

This man reports that he has found twenty-odd things that can be done to make a group of people more comfortable. Most of them can be managed without anyone noticing —and he is particular about this, for he doesn't want to seem to be a bustling busybody.

"Frequently I get a smile of appreciation from a hostess," he says, "but my real reward is that my self-consciousness has disappeared. The reason, of course, is that I am no longer thinking of myself and my own comfort."

Chapter 30

Neighborhood-Giving

I have discovered that there are many ways one can give himself to his neighborhood or community, with small expenditures of time or effort.

For example, the traffic light at the top of a certain hill in my neighborhood changed so quickly that if as many as four cars were waiting for the green light, it turned back to red before the fourth car could get through. Everybody was cussing that light, but no one was doing anything about it.

Here was an opportunity to do a bit of neighborhood-giving. I wrote a note to the Police Department calling attention to the situation. By the next afternoon the green-light interval had been lengthened.

Another example: One evening at a dinner party someone told the distressing situation of a woman living on one of the heavily traveled streets of our town who was dying. Every time a heavy truck or bus went over a hump in the macadam pavement in front of her house, the resulting vibration shook her bed and caused her acute distress.

The next morning I called the Commissioner of Streets and explained the situation. Before nightfall a paving crew had leveled that hump. Not only the patient, but all of her neighbors and friends were relieved, for they had suffered for her.

These two experiences taught me this important lesson in community affairs: Never assume that anything wrong has to *stay* that way. It is an old saying that what is everybody's business is nobody's business. Whenever anything in the everybody's-business category comes to my attention, I do whatever I can about it. I have found endless opportunities.

✓ ✓ ✓

Driving to the office one morning, I noticed a metal hoop in the middle of the road. I started to steer around it. Then my impulse-habit prodded me into action. Pulling over to the curb, I got out and picked up the hoop and tossed it into a safe place, before its sharp edges could cut some motorist's tire.

Half an hour later a stranger came up to me in the Post Office. "I just want to say that I wish there were more citizens as thoughtful as you," he said. "I saw you pick up that hoop. After this I'm never going to drive past such hazards. Thanks for waking me up."

That is another fine thing about giving yourself away: You may be starting a *chain* of giving-away.

✓ ✓ ✓

Walking along a country road in New England one Sunday morning with a friend, I observed that whenever we came to an unsightly piece of paper, a pasteboard box or a bottle, he would pick it up and toss it over the stone wall, out of sight.

"I appointed myself a Roadside Pickup Committee of One

many years ago," this man explained, "and it has been great fun."

I soon found myself clearing one side of the road while he cleared the other. All the rest of the summer, every time I traveled that road, its neatness gave me special pleasure. In my walks in the country I now pick up as I go, and find it makes my strolls more enjoyable.

✓   ✓   ✓

These are all negative examples; but there are plenty of positive ways a citizen of goodwill can give to his city or town or village.

A printer in a western town was annoyed by the crudely hand-lettered signs in the windows and on the doors of many of the retail stores explaining that they were closed on Wednesday afternoons.

"Those crude signs are a disgrace to this town," he complained to his wife.

"Well," she asked, "why don't you furnish the merchants with neatly printed signs—with your compliments? Wouldn't it be good advertising for you?"

"That's a fine idea," he said. The very next day he printed three sizes of "Closed Wednesday Afternoon" signs and sent a set to each merchant, offering to supply, gratis, as many additional sets as might be needed.

He didn't even put his advertisement on the signs. "I don't care whether anybody remembers that I printed them," he told his wife. "I'm getting a kick out of seeing how much I have improved the appearance of the stores of this town!"

The last I heard he was looking for other ways he could use inexpensive forms of printing to dress up the town so that as a printer he could take pride in it. My guess is he has found them, for once you make a hobby of giving yourself to your community, you will almost trip over opportunities.

✓ ✓ ✓

A woman writer in a Southern city was bemoaning the fact that when new people moved into the community it took a long time for anybody to find out anything about them, and even longer for them to begin to feel at home.

"Why don't you introduce them to the town?" her husband asked.

"I would if I knew how," she replied.

A week later an idea came to her. She stopped in to see the editor of the local paper and volunteered to call at the homes of all newcomers and write a few paragraphs about them, to be run in a weekly column, "Introducing Our New Citizens."

The editor agreed enthusiastically. The woman now visits each new family, finds out where they come from, the names and ages of their children, what the husband does, their college, church and fraternal affiliations, their hobbies, anything and everything they are willing to tell that will help to introduce them to the community. Probably no feature in the Saturday issue is as popular.

✓ ✓ ✓

I noticed that a commuter living in a Chicago suburb seemed to know everybody on the station platform. During the course of conversation with him one morning he told me that he did know just about everybody in town.

"For years I've made it a point to watch for strange faces

and give them a 'good morning,'" he explained, "so they will feel that they know *someone* in their new home town. It has made many fine friends for my wife and me."

I thought of Robert Louis Stevenson's saying, "A friend is a present you give yourself."

Then there is the neighborhood aspect of giving to the community.

One night when my wife and I were feeling lonely, I suggested that we call on some neighbors up the street.

"Oh, they are probably busy with their friends," she objected. "They don't want to be bothered by a lonely couple like us."

"Let's find out," I said, going to the phone.

"Are you folks doing anything special tonight?" I asked.

"George and I have been sitting here feeling terribly lonesome, and wishing there was someone to play bridge with," came the reply.

"Well, there is—will you come to our house, or shall we come to yours?"

I don't know when two lonely couples ever had a more enjoyable evening!

If there were a little blue light over every door, which lit up automatically as a sort of S.O.S. call when the family felt lonely, I wonder if Lonesome Lights wouldn't be burning in many houses on every street, and many apartments in every big apartment house, nearly every evening.

*   *   *

The late Harry B. Hostetter copied his neighborhood-giving hobby from the famous Johnny Appleseed who planted apple trees over a large area many years ago. Hostetter's specialty was planting acorns. He put a handful of them in his pocket whenever he went for a walk, and planted one in any spot where he thought it had a chance to grow and mature.

He got enjoyment from looking at hundreds of oaks which grew from acorns he had planted twenty years before, some of them six inches or more in diameter, and forty feet tall.

This man gave not only to his own generation, but to future generations. And why not? We inherited the fine old trees we enjoy; why shouldn't we pay our debt to our grandfathers by making the world a more beautiful place for our grandchildren?

The world would be a cleaner, safer, happier, more attractive place if each of us were to adopt some neighborhood-giving specialty of his own. We would find plenty of opportunities to practice it, for not a city, town, or hamlet in the world is as friendly, beautiful, or livable as it *might* be—and which we could make it.

Chapter 31

Giving-Away Parking Spaces

A novel form of giving-away has been worked out by one of my correspondents, a retired man with plenty of time on his hands. He wrote:

Parking a car has become the Big National Vexation in cities, towns and suburbs. It took me a long time to wake up to the fact that parking spaces are another gift that I could make. In this case to complete strangers, whom I probably never would even see.

He went on to explain that one Saturday morning he had slipped into the only vacant space in front of a grocery store in his suburban shopping section with only curb-side parking, and was congratulating himself on his good fortune in finding such a convenient place to park. He continued:

As I got out of my car I noticed the disappointment in the face of an elderly woman in the car just behind me. I realized now that she, too, had been heading for this empty space. But I had been ahead of her. She would now have to prowl for a vacant space.

"If I'd only known," I told myself, "I'd have been glad to leave the space for her. But you can't know about such situations."

As I came out of the grocery store a few minutes later I noticed a number of women carrying heavy bags of groceries, heading up and down the street to their cars, some of which were probably a block or more away.

"Why couldn't I often give a convenient parking space to my fellow citizens?" I asked myself. "Just never try to park close to a store or the Post Office or the Library. Leave the empty space that I might have for someone who may really need to be parked nearby."

✓ ✓ ✓

Being a man of action, my correspondent reported that from that day on, unless he has had something heavy to carry, he has passed up an empty parking space convenient to his errand, and sometimes driven as much as two or three blocks to park.

Occasionally when he has walked by the empty space he had passed up—"given to some stranger"—he would see small children or an elderly person waiting in the car parked there, and he felt sure someone was most grateful for the "gift" of the parking space.

✓ ✓ ✓

Presently it occurred to him that it wasn't necessary to know who the beneficiary might be in order to enjoy, deep down inside of himself, the fun of being thoughtful of his neighbors. In a talk with him he told me:

"Then, one morning when I had to drive three long blocks along a residential side street to park when I had passed a most convenient empty space," he said, "I made an interesting discovery. In your book you stress that we can't possibly give ourselves away without getting back more than we give. It was a beautiful June morning and I was thinking about this as I stepped along briskly drinking in the fresh spring air. 'I'm having a most enjoyable walk,' I told myself. Which reminded me that my doctor had urged me to get more outdoor exercise. Well, I was getting it!

"Since then, whenever I park two or three (and sometimes more) blocks from my destination—*I take a walk.* Head up. Shoulders back. Arms swinging. Breathing deeply. Feeling alive!

"I had discovered that to walk *voluntarily,* rather than with a sense of *compulsion,* is employing practical psychology that turns parking frustration into beneficial exercise!"

Since my talk with this thoughtful man I have often given away parking spaces in this fashion. And I have enjoyed being an anonymous parking-space Santa Claus. Not to mention benefiting from the exercise.

✦ ✦ ✦

For some time I thought this giving-plan would not work in shopping center or municipal parking lots. But I discovered that one can often give *thoughtfulness* in such places by alerting a looker-for-space as you walk toward your car to the fact that your space will be available, motioning them to follow you.

I have myself been given parking space in this fashion, and have been grateful.

"Parking empathy," you might call this whole idea. Certainly it is a thoughtful form of neighborliness.

Chapter 32

On Being a Credit-Giver

One of the best-liked and most successful men I know has a giving-specialty. He goes out of his way to *give credit*.

In his business he gives credit for every job well done, for every good idea suggested, for particularly prompt service, for a well-written letter, for intelligent handling of a situation. This he does not only directly to the person involved, but in the presence of others whenever possible.

He gives his wife credit, before the children, for the many thoughtful things she does, so that they will acquire the habit of credit-giving. He gives the children credit, in the presence of one another, for anything they do that shows care or thoughtfulness or enterprise.

He gives the maid credit for the tasty dishes she prepares.

In his community he not only writes notes of appreciation to members of the city administration whenever anything they do pleases him, but takes pains to give them credit before his neighbors and friends.

In his church he is constantly on the lookout for some fine piece of work by a committee member, or a thoughtful service someone has performed, to mention it appreciatively, in public if possible.

When asked by one of his less gracious associates whether giving credit did not swell some people's heads, he replied laughingly, "Sure—one in fifty, perhaps. But such people would swell up anyway, and life takes care of swelled heads quite effectively. I'm interested in the other forty-nine."

I've added credit-giving to my collection!

Gifts-of-credit are, I discover, appreciated by everyone, no matter how old or how young, how great or how small. Yet most of us neglect many opportunities to make others experience the warm glow that comes from spoken recognition of the jobs they have done well.

Just another case of too much taking-for-granted.

Chapter 33

On the Sharing of Surpluses

Up to now the giving-away we have discussed has not involved money or material things, beyond a sheet of note
paper and a postage stamp, a phone call, or the expenditure
of a trifling sum.

There are, however, two or three exceptions to this rule.
I believe, for example, that surplus things of all kinds should
be shared. If you have more of something than you can presently use, whether it be a barrel of apples or a basket of
tomatoes, more hats than you need, only half-worn automobile tires that you will probably never use, a superabundance
of flowers or vegetables in your garden—a surplus of anything at all—you will probably get far greater pleasure from
sharing it than from hoarding it.

✓   ✓   ✓

One year I spent Christmas Day with a bachelor friend
in his apartment in Cambridge, Massachusetts. Among his
Christmas gifts was a box of a dozen sterling silver teaspoons,
sent him by his sister, who knew that he got his own breakfasts and occasionally served a meal to his bachelor cronies.

No sooner had he opened the box of teaspoons than he

went to the cupboard in his kitchenette and got out a dozen silver-plated teaspoons. Calling the janitor's wife, he asked her to come up to the apartment. When she appeared he presented her with the plated teaspoons. She was delighted.

"I might possibly need those spoons some time," he explained to me, "but I don't need them now—and with her large family she does need them."

This spontaneous action awoke me to a realization that, as far as our happiness is concerned, we are living *now*—not tomorrow or next week or next year. If all of us were to share our present surpluses, we should probably find that our future needs would be taken care of in good time.

✓ ✓ ✓

In the world's attics, basements, cupboards, and bureau drawers are millions of dollars' worth of perfectly good things —furniture, clothing, linens, curtains, tools, toys, baby things, luggage, electrical equipment, cooking utensils, porch and garden furniture—just taking up room and collecting dust year after year. They are not serving us, and in most cases might better be given to someone who can use them *now*.

One of my neighbors, a widow with a large house furnished to the point of overcrowdedness, recently started to give away everything she was not using. And what joy she still is getting out of presenting these things to needy people, young couples just setting up housekeeping, friends, relatives, and neighbors!

I watched her as she presented one of her neighbors with a length of garden hose. She did not make the mistake of doing it in a "Lady Bountiful" spirit.

"I wonder if you can use this section of garden hose," she said. "I have more hose than I can possibly use. When it is coiled up in the garage the coil is so big it's in the way. . . . No; I couldn't think of accepting anything for it. I just want to feel that it is being useful to someone."

*   *   *

My Uncle Ed owned an unusual mustache cup and saucer, designed for use by a left-handed person. Uncle Ed was not interested in collecting mustache cups, so this one was stored in a box in his attic.

For years he tried to sell it to a man who had a very fine collection, but no left-handed ones. The collector, a man of modest means, could not afford the price he asked for it.

"Why don't you give it to him, and have the pleasure of thinking of that cup ocupying a place of honor in his collection?" I once asked my uncle.

"Give it to him?" he snorted. "I paid six dollars for it twenty years ago, and it must be worth much more now."

When Uncle Ed was in his last illness he sent for the collector and gave him the cup. "I've hated myself for holding out for my price all these years," he told him, "I realize now that I've been cheating myself as well as you."

This incident reminded me of Axel Munthe's wise observation about money and material things: "What you keep to yourself you lose, what you give away you keep forever."

*   *   *

The most individual example of surplus-sharing I have ever encountered was the sharing of a talent. One day I met a well-known author on the street in New York. "What are you writing now?" I asked.

"I'm writing a book for my maiden sister," he replied. "I have enough royalties rolling in to take care of me and my family. So I'm going to assign the royalties on this book—large or small as they may be—to her, though I haven't told her yet. I'm having a grand time working on her surprise book!"

✓ ✓ ✓

Most of us have surpluses of one sort or another which we could share. And after all, as Norma S. Scholl writes: "Everything we have is really *loaned* to us; we can't take anything with us when we depart. If we have no use for a thing, we should pass it on to someone else who can use it—*now*."

Chapter 34

An Army of Anonymous Givers

A letter in my mail one morning opened my eyes to the fact that right in our own communities all of us have an example of the wonderful effectiveness of self-giving. The letter in question read:

It was ten years ago that I first read your book, but I sort of tossed it aside the same as I had other "inspirational" books. At the time I was searching for a way out of a terrible drinking problem. I went through twelve years of hell before I surrendered. Your book played a great part, believe me.

Then, when I came into Alcoholics Anonymous, I suddenly saw the tie-in: that we must give of ourselves in order to receive, and the more we give the more we receive.

I immediately went back to your book and it opened up a new day to me. I have given away many copies since, and I never can keep one myself!

Certainly the members of Alcoholics Anonymous are a band of dedicated givers of their time, their experience, and their understanding. To which they add faith and hope and courage—three of the greatest gifts one man or woman can give to a fellow human being.

Chapter 35

The Gracious Art of Receiving

In an article in *The Reader's Digest* describing that unforgettable character Edward Sheldon, Anne Morrow Lindbergh wrote: "He knew how to receive so graciously that the gift was enhanced by its reception. It was the rarest pleasure to bring things to him. . . . Warmed by his welcome, how beautiful became the things one brought to him."

To be a really successful giver-away it is necessary, also, to study the art of graceful and generous receiving. "To receive a present handsomely and in the right spirit," wrote Leigh Hunt a century ago, "even when you have none to return, is to give one in return."

If you find pleasure in giving, so do others. You have only to stop and think how you feel when your giving is rebuffed or looked upon with suspicion, or when someone is slow to enter into the spirit of it, to realize how important it is to accept and acknowledge graciously the thoughtfulnesses of others toward you.

The act of giving strikes a tiny spark which, if the receiver is quick to react, starts a fire glowing in two hearts. If the spark is allowed to die, part of the glow is lost to both.

Sincere compliments are among the finest gifts we can make, the most hungered for, and the most appreciated by nearly all of us. Yet how few of us have learned to receive a compliment gracefully. Instead, we too often clumsily bat it back by making an awkward disclaimer which spoils the pleasure for both parties.

Among all of the people I know, I have observed that a young married niece, who goes through life receiving compliments on her prettiness, her talents, her clothes, her children, and her home, has most completely mastered the art of receiving compliments, and doing it without the least trace of self-complacency. Giving her a compliment is always an enjoyable experience.

A study of her technique reveals it to be simple indeed. First, a quick smile of appreciation. Then an equally quick "Thank you," followed by some phrase that takes the spotlight off herself. For example, "Yes, *isn't* it a pretty dress. Mother sent it to me." Or, "I got the idea for rearranging this room from So-and-So's new book on interior decorating."

Her secret is that she never keeps compliments to herself, though she admits that she thrives on them. But she accepts them for a fleeting second—and then passes them on.

Whether we are giving compliments or presents or sharing surpluses, all of us like our gifts to be received graciously, but not selfishly. Again my niece provides the pattern. She is as generous in giving compliments to others as she is gracious in receiving them. While she never makes the mistake of trying to pass a compliment right back, on a clumsy quid pro quo basis, she does watch for a later opportunity to return it, when it will not seem like barter. She believes in keeping her Compliment Account balanced.

Receiving, like giving, must be kept *fresh*. All the fun is killed for the giver if his or her gift is taken for granted. The fact that I have received the same kind of a gift from a person before, does not entitle me to assume that my appreciation is understood and need not be expressed again. It is my feeling that we have no right to take for granted that even members of our family know that we appreciate the things they give us or do for us, no matter how often repeated. All of us like to be *told* that our gifts are appreciated.

In an affluent age it is all too easy to take gifts for granted. Recently at lunch a business associate remarked that he and his wife had given their teen-age daughter fifty dollars for extra vacation spending money, outside of her regular allowance, "And she didn't even thank us," he said. Then he added, "We know she did appreciate it, but by not expressing her appreciation she took some of the fun out of our little surprise gift."

✓ ✓ ✓

A little touch of ceremony is never amiss in connection with giving and receiving, no matter how simple the gift or how expected. I know an elderly gentleman who goes out to the garden every summer morning, picks a single bloom of whatever is in flower, and takes it to his invalid wife. The smile on her face as he presents it to her, and her exclamation of pleasure, are so genuine that an outsider would assume this was the first such attention she had ever received; yet the little ceremony is thirty summers old.

✓ ✓ ✓

Years ago I learned that a "second thanks" is an important part of the gracious art of receiving. If a person sends me a book and I cannot read it immediately, I write a note of appreciation at the time. Later—and it may be many months, for I have much reading to do—when I finish the book I write a second note, telling the giver of my enjoyment, this time in specific terms.

Recently I had the pleasure of being on the receiving end of a second thanks. Four years ago I gave one of my nephews a metallurgical handbook as a birthday present, for which he thanked me appropriately at the time. Recently I received a letter from him saying that he had changed his job, and that in his new work he had occasion to refer almost daily to the handbook I had given him. He wanted me to know how useful my gift was proving.

This note made so favorable an impression on me that I now have my eye peeled for other books to send this appreciative young man.

✓ ✓ ✓

The second thanks idea is by no means confined to gifts of books. It is as broad as giving and receiving. And here, again, acting on impulse helps to make life much more interesting.

Some time ago a friend sent me an ingenious aluminum lime squeezer. One summer evening when my family was away I used it to make myself a cool drink. As I sat on the porch sipping the drink, I felt a surge of appreciation for my friend's thoughtfulness in sending me the handy gadget.

"Why not *tell* him?" I asked myself. I went to the phone and called him up.

"I just used that tricky lime squeezer you gave me, to make a cold drink," I said. "I thought I'd call you up and tell you how much I am enjoying that gadget. . . . Yes, my family is away. . . . Yours too? *Well, come on over!*"

Ten minutes later John arrived. What had started out to be a lonesome evening for each of us turned into a thoroughly enjoyable one for both of us.

If you were to take stock right now of the nice things that have been given to you, or done for you, for which you have already expressed your appreciation once, you would probably find that you are still enjoying a number of them. If you are not already an habitual second-thanker, why not take the trouble to tell the givers—again—of your pleasure? They will appreciate it; and you will refresh your own spirit by *re-appreciating* their gift.

Chapter 36

The Investment of Influence

Years ago Newell Dwight Hillis, when pastor of Plymouth Congregational Church in Brooklyn, wrote a stimulating little book entitled *The Investment of Influence*. It has been out of print for many years, but it has never been out of my mind. Its theme was that every individual is richer and more powerful than he thinks.

Each of us, no matter how humble our situation, has at least a small circle of friends and acquaintances who are influenced, consciously or unconsciously, by our ideas, our example, our character. Daily, in our contacts with them, we are giving ourselves to them, whether we realize it or not.

A small act that costs us little in time or effort may make the day supremely happy for some person in this group. An unconscious giving of ourselves, in tolerance or loyalty to a friend or neighbor, may carry him through a tight place. A word of encouragement from us, at just the right moment, may alter the entire life of someone who looks up to us to an extent we do not realize.

Then there is the matter of building up our friends and working associates.

Many years ago Elihu Root wrote: "I observe that there

are two entirely different theories according to which individual men seek to get on in the world. One theory leads a man to pull down everybody around him in order to climb up on them to a higher place. The other leads a man to help everybody around him in order that he may go up with them."

It is so easy to use our influence to pull people down, by belittling their achievements, pointing out their weaknesses (and who of us is without his weaknesses?), and undermining their characters by spreading gossip. In so doing we belittle ourselves, and lose the respect of people who are too big to stoop to such things.

Whereas, when we do everything in our power to build up other people, we build ourselves too, in character and reputation, and in our own self-respect.

✓   ✓   ✓

You and I belong a little to the neighborhood in which we live, a little to our city or town and state, a little to our country, and at least a tiny bit to all humanity.

It is a mistake, therefore, for us to concentrate our influence by too narrowly confining our giving-away, for if we concentrate on giving to family and close friends we are shortchanging the world. Furthermore, we are missing the joy of sharing ourselves broadly, and we are using only a fraction of our giving-muscles.

But perhaps the most important reason for not concentrating our giving-away on a few people is that it tends to make them selfish, which is as great a disservice as one human being can do to others. Not only does it deny them the pleasure of giving themselves, by making them chronic receivers, but it undermines their self-respect.

So, when people grow used to your gifts of yourself and begin to demand them, it is time to stop giving so much to those particular people. This may wake them up to their self-centeredness—and such an awakening is in itself a valuable gift.

Therefore be wise. Spread your giving-away over a constantly widening circle of friends, relatives, business or professional associates, acquaintances, neighbors—yes, and strangers. To do so will extend your influence in an ever-widening circle, enriching the lives of many people.

Chapter 37

For Teenagers Only
(Parents Not Invited In)

I have made an interesting discovery about young people. Once they get the idea, they are often better givers-away than grown-ups. Since they have so many uses for their spending money, they have to figure on giving *themselves*. So they think up ways that would never occur to older people.

Then, too, young people are more impulsive. They have fewer inhibitions; they are less apt to be afraid of being snubbed. They think of something nice to do for someone and *do* it. And that is the real secret of being good at giving-away: to act on a generous impulse before it has time to cool.

The best place to start your giving-away is right at home. After all, you are a member of the family—of the home "Establishment." If you accept that responsibility in a spirit of family cooperation, your parents are likely to be more open-minded about such changes as you think should be made in your home and family life.

The world is changing so rapidly these days that all the members of *every* family need to meet the multiple problems of living together by giving to each other understanding and tolerance, in a spirit of *mutual* adaptability. For the giving cannot be all one-sided.

Being constantly asked or told to do things around the house or for the family is a bore. But it is also the cue to some Grade A ideas for giving yourself to your parents. It is only necessary to do—voluntarily—many of the things you know you *ought* to do or that you are going to *have* to do eventually anyway, to give your parents some gifts that will please them more than you can possibly realize.

✓ ✓ ✓

For instance, you can help *cheerfully* with the housework, weed the garden, mow the lawn, and do many other chores.

You can keep your room picked up (if you don't already) and save your mother much time and energy.

You can do your school homework or your practicing without having to be nagged. (This would be a marvelous gift in many a home, for it wears parents out to have to keep after their youngsters.)

You can help keep the car washed and polished, so it will be a credit to the family. And you can be thoughtful about asking to use it—for parents have their plans, too.

You can keep sensible night hours, and by so doing relieve your parents of much anxiety—and nothing ages them as fast as anxiety.

You can help with the care of the younger children, so that your mother will be able to rest, or do some of the things she never seems to have time for.

If you don't think of these things as being "gifts" to your parents, it is because you are so full of energy that you don't realize how tired older people get, and how little time they have to do the things *they* would like to do.

Perhaps none of the things I have mentioned represent

your particular opportunities for giving yourself to your family. You know better than I what you could do to make it a happier family.

It is not the *doing* of these things that is a gift, so much as it is the promptness and cheerfulness with which you do them. It is the *spirit* in which each member of the family carries on that makes any home a livable "Establishment."

1   1   1

Teenagers can give in dozens of ways to their brothers and sisters, as well as to their parents. All they have to do is to think of the kind of things they would appreciate having their brothers and sisters do for them.

In *Your Life,* Marion Simms told the story of a very small girl who wanted to give her older sister a birthday gift but had no money to buy her one. But that didn't stump her. When big sister opened her birthday packages at breakfast, she found an envelope tied with a ribbon. Inside were three colored slips of paper, each with a gift neatly printed on it:

>Good for 2 dish washings.
>Good for 2 bed makings.
>Good for 2 kitchen floor scrubbings.

These three presents were among her most welcome birthday surprises.

1   1   1

There is probably one catch that may make you hesitate about cheerfully volunteering to do things around the house. Because you are so willing, the family may come to expect you to be available for chores every minute of the time you are home.

As I look back at my own youth, I know I felt that my time was not properly respected by my parents and my older brothers and sister. Being the youngest of four children, I was constantly being asked to do this or that, often just when I had other plans that were important to me.

I realize now that part of the fault was my own. Because I put off doing the things I was asked to do, or that I knew very well I should do, I let myself in for being reminded of them—even nagged into doing them—usually at the most inconvenient times. If I had my teens to live over again, I would proposition my parents along this line:

"If you will tell me the chores that I am supposed to do as my share of running the house, and I promise to do them without your having to keep after me, may I have the rest of my time to myself?" I believe most parents would be more than happy to make this kind of a bargain.

I would then organize those chores to get them out of the way early, so they wouldn't be hanging over me. But I wouldn't stop there: I would work in little surprise gifts-of-myself to the family as often as possible. And I am sure that it would not be difficult to work them in, along with my regular chores.

✓ ✓ ✓

Of course, you need not limit your giving to your family.

When you have spare time you can offer to run errands or do chores for your neighbors.

At school you can give yourself to your teachers, not by bringing apples or being sissy, but by giving your close attention during class, by having your homework ready on time, by being helpful in any or every way that occurs to you.

You can give to your pals by going over their homework with them when there is something they do not understand —but never by doing it *for* them.

You can give to your scout master, your athletic coach, your teammates, by acting on every helpful or generous impulse that comes to you in your association with them.

✦ ✦ ✦

It is never too early to start giving yourself away. Some time ago a California boy named Jerry wrote me the following letter:

I'm a kid 13 years of age. I wash dishes for my parents in a sandwich shop. When there are no dishes, I grab *The Reader's Digest* and sit down to read. I read your article "Try Giving Yourself Away." I'm not only going to make a *hobby* of giving myself away—I'm going to make it *a part of my life.*

You say take an idea while it's "hot." "To be successful at it one must act fast, while the impulse is fresh." I got the idea of writing to you this afternoon, I'm writing tonight, 9:30—as "hot" as I can get it!

Starting at thirteen to make giving himself away a part of his life, Jerry will "go places." He is sure to have an interesting life, and to make a host of friends. I wish I had started at thirteen!

✦ ✦ ✦

Every time you give a bit of yourself you plant a little seed of Future Happiness. All the rest of your life these seeds will keep springing up unexpectedly along your path.

When you need a friend to give you a lift in some situation, likely as not along will come a person for whom you did something thoughtful when you were a youngster.

By taking up giving-away as a hobby in your teens you will develop an interesting and lively personality—gracious, friendly, thoughtful, and *unexpected!*

Chapter 38

Concerning Rebuffs

People ask me, "Do you never meet with rebuffs in your giving-away?"

Yes; every now and then I receive a snub from someone. Occasionally, too, I encounter a person so cynical that he or she eyes me with suspicion, or rejects my giving entirely.

What of it? We suffer plenty of rebuffs in our *getting*, but we do not stop trying to earn a living on that account. We even expect to have to swallow our pride at times. Why should we not be just as willing to do a bit of pride-swallowing when we are trying to earn happiness for ourselves by *giving*? After all, we work at both for the same ultimate reason—to get enjoyment out of living.

Some people are so selfish, and so lacking in common courtesy, that they resent others who are generous and thoughtful, and willing to give themselves. One man wrote me:

I couldn't believe at first that you were really sincere in what you tried to do for me. I kept looking for an ulterior motive. But I have come to realize that you were entirely unselfish. I am thoroughly ashamed of my boorish attitude. I am going to try out your philosophy myself. I think maybe you have what I've been looking for all these years—but looking in the wrong direction, I now see.

Some rebuffs are inevitable, and they even have their usefulness. Once you make up your mind to this, your timidity and thin-skinnedness will wither away. You will find yourself grinning on those occasions when you bump into a person who meets your giving with suspicion or rudeness. When you reach this point, you will have graduated from the amateur class.

✓   ✓   ✓

Acting on a giving-impulse, a woman in Ohio wrote a letter of appreciation to the author of a book which had deeply moved her. She received no reply and was very much put out. After reading *Try Giving Yourself Away,* she wrote: "I had resolved never to do any more of that sort of letter writing. Most of my efforts have either met with indifference, been laughed at, or were received with a sophistication that merely implied, 'Another scalp.' "

The trouble with this woman is that she has been doing her giving-away in a spirit of barter. Admittedly it is a pleasure to receive a letter in return. But if I receive no reply I do not take it as a rebuff.

Since writers, artists, musicians, and stage celebrities are gifted people whose ego feeds on appreciation and applause, I am willing to add my bit of fuel to the flame of their genius, not for their sakes alone, but so that they may be encouraged to give the world still more of themselves. If they write books that give me pleasure, for instance, I want them to write more books, so that I may continue to enjoy their art. Should not all who make life enjoyable be encouraged?

Having dealt in ideas all my business life, I sometimes try to give manufacturers and merchants ideas for their advertising, for new products, for improving their service. Always I offer them "with no strings attached."

In a few instances my ideas have been accepted in the spirit in which they were offered. But more often I receive a letter of rejection. The first such letter seemed like a slap in the face, until the legal counsel for a large manufacturing concern explained to me that his company received many letters from people suggesting new products, or improvements in old products, or outlining advertising ideas.

"It is rarely that these ideas have not already occurred to someone in our company," he explained, "and if they are good, oftener than not we are working on them. If we express any interest, we are likely to let ourselves in for a claim that we have 'stolen' the correspondent's idea. In several instances we have been sued for large sums. So we are obliged, politely but firmly, to decline practically all the ideas that are sent us, even though it seems ungracious."

I could see his point. But I still try to give away business ideas occasionally. And once in a while I have the satisfaction of seeing one used.

✦   ✦   ✦

Nor is the field of ideas the only one in which you will occasionally meet seeming rebuffs. You might just as well make up your mind to it that some of your gifts-of-yourself will fall flat

So do some of the carefully planned jokes of the top television comedians. But do they give up their TV careers because of that? By no means. Nor do they blame the TV audience. Their attitude is that they have set out to earn their living by entertaining people, and it is up to them to find out how to "put over" their lines. They experiment with facial expressions, tone of voice, emphasis, timing, as well as with the lines themselves.

✦ ✦ ✦

One evening I was backstage at a performance of a very successful Broadway comedy. At one point all the members of the cast who were not in the scene then being played gathered in the wings and attentively watched and listened. Suddenly the audience burst into a "belly-laugh." The assembled players exchanged delighted glances.

The stage manager explained to me that the particular line which had brought the laugh had of late been failing to go over. The company had discussed it and decided that the star had unconsciously changed the inflection of a single word, thus altering the whole sense of the line. So this evening he had tried changing the inflection, and their theory had proved correct.

"That's what makes the theater interesting," explained the stage manager. "If entertaining the public were *too* easy, we'd all get bored!"

Practice, persistence, and experimentation are required in any art. The art of giving-away is no exception. If our self-giving were surefire with every person and in every situation, it would be too easy to be fun.

A final word of warning: *Don't take your giving-away too seriously.*

Keep your sense of humor in good working order at all times. Add a whimsical touch, or a dash of merriment if you feel a bit self-conscious, or if you half-way anticipate a rebuff. A good-natured laugh is a priceless gift in many a situation. Remember, you are trying to make the world a brighter, merrier, more exciting place. Sanctimoniousness is definitely OUT.

Chapter 39

The Fun Comes from Inside

Let me be utterly honest: There are a few people who will *not* find greater happiness in taking up giving-away as a hobby. They will, in fact, scoff at the idea, and make fun of this book.

This will not bother me in the least, any more than I should be bothered if my hobby happened to be collecting sea shells or Russian icons and some people thought it a silly hobby. We collectors have our fun *inside;* we are not dependent on the approval of outsiders.

Most of the scoffers will be men and women who are convinced that getting their own way, getting the best of every bargain, getting credit for everything they do, getting ahead at the expense of other people—in short, "getting theirs"—is the only sensible way to go through life.

They are the people who absorb all the compliments you give them, but never give any in return; who always let you reach for the check; who criticize other people yet deeply resent any criticism of themselves; who expect others to go out of their way to do things for them, but never volunteer to do anything in return.

They are the world's absorbers. Their whole philosophy

of life is to Get-Get-Get. They do not know the meaning of the word GIVE.

Such people are apt to discover, too late, that an all-getting life is only *half* living.

✦ ✦ ✦

Then there is the kind of person William Hazlitt described in one of his essays:

There are persons who cannot make friends. Who are they? Those who cannot be friends. It is not the want of understanding or good nature, of entertaining or useful qualities, that you complain of: On the contrary, they have probably many points of attraction; but they have one that neutralizes all these—they care nothing about you, and are neither the better nor worse for what you think of them. They manifest no joy at your approach; and when you leave them it is with a feeling that they can do just as well without you. This is not sullenness, nor indifference, nor absence of mind; but they are intent solely on their own thoughts, and you are merely one of the subjects they exercise them upon. They live in society as in a solitude; and, however their brain works, their pulse beats neither faster nor slower for the common accidents of life.

Such people will not be interested in giving-away as a hobby. They lack the capacity to "glow." Greater happiness cannot be guaranteed them.

✦ ✦ ✦

Finally, there are those who are slow to *believe* what, deep inside of them, they *know* about life; that it *is* "more blessed to give than to receive." For this group there is hope. Given time, and a bit of experimentation, many of them will one day work through their skepticism and become givers.

The fact is, I do not recommend giving-away as a hobby to anyone who is not prepared to keep at it long enough to discover that the enjoyment is in the giving, and that any return that may come, over and above the inner glow, is in the nature of an extra dividend. I do not recommend it any more than skiing can be recommended as a sport for a person who gives up after the first two or three spills, and is not willing to persevere until that wonderful moment when he suddenly gets the hang of it—and goes skimming down the slope, with the whole wide world seeming to cooperate to give him a thrill!

But of this I am certain: Any person of sincerity and good will, who will persevere in giving himself away more generously than he has ever thought of doing up to this minute, will enjoy a *much* happier life from then on.

Chapter 40

Perspective on our Troubled Times

Never, within the memory of any of us, have the times been so troubled. Much that we read, and most of the news on radio and TV, tends to increase our confusion and concern.

Following is a paragraph which I came upon recently in my reading: "Our earth is degenerate in these latter days. Bribery and corruption are common. Children no longer obey their parents . . . The end of the world evidently approaches."

I shook my head. This was the gloomiest yet, I told myself. Then I read a footnote: "The above doleful observation was translated from an Assyrian Tablet dated 2800 B.C."

The world has survived for almost five thousand years since that observation was written! Through wars and revolutions; through plagues and natural calamities; through man-made booms and depressions; through "hell and high water."

The world is always going through what historian Arnold Toynbee has described as "the painfulness of being human." This phrase gives us a clue to hope.

Few of us are in a position of authority or influence to cure the big troubles that press in on the world. But all of us can do our personal bit toward relieving some of the "painfulness" of being "human."

We can be *helpfully* human, *understandingly* human, even *hopefully* human, in our dealings with those around us. This is merely the essence of self-giving.

✓   ✓   ✓

I am sometimes accused of being an optimist, as though that were stupid in such threatening times. To which I reply that if this means being a Pollyanna optimist, I plead *not guilty*. I realize that we *can* stupidly blow up this planet. But after reading the last sentence of the complaint on the Assyrian Tablet of 2800 B.C.—"The end of the world evidently approaches"—I refuse to surrender to any such fatalistic end of human life.

I do plead *guilty,* however, to being a giving-and-doing optimist. I believe we can all give of ourselves in many, many ways every day, that will help to humanize the small corner of the world in which we live and work.

But we can't permit ourselves to be sitting-around-waiting optimists. We must be *doing* optimists. Nothing so swiftly lifts one's spirit as to stop worrying and *start doing* anything and everything we possibly can about the near-at-hand problems and troubles, of our friends and neighbors, our communities.

Doing reflects our faith in the worthiness of humanity, and our hope in the future.

Friendliness. Faith. Hope. These are three great gifts-of-ourselves. They are the bracing tonic the whole world needs in these troubled times!

Chapter 41

Greater Happiness for All of Us
(Beginning Right Away!)

Some wise person has written: "Success is a journey, not a destination. Happiness is to be found along the way, not at the end of the road—for then the journey is over and it is too late. The time for happiness is today, not tomorrow."

If we wait to *arrive* at happiness, we shall be sadly disappointed in life. Happiness must be experienced as we journey, a minute here, an hour there, occasionally a day, once in a long while several days or a month.

But the months and weeks and days and hours are all made up of minutes, and if we live for happy minutes the hours and days and weeks and months will take care of themselves. We shall find our road through life a pleasant one, and spend less time worrying about the distant goal.

A stream of happiness-opportunities is flowing past us continuously, during the hours we spend at home, in the office or store or shop or laboratory where we work, as we walk along the street, as we drive hither and yon, as we travel by train or plane or bus—in short, wherever we are and whatever we are doing.

We would do well to adopt this creed, written a century ago by Stephen Grellet: "I expect to pass through this world but ònce. Any good therefore that I can do, or any kindness that I can show to any fellow creature, let me do it now. Let me not defer or neglect it, for I shall not pass this way again.'

✓   ✓   ✓

We permit too many opportunities for happiness to slip by us because we labor under two major delusions.

One of these delusions is that we shall be happy WHEN—

When we arrive at a certain destination

When we can be with a certain person or in a certain place

When our schooling is finished

When we get a better job

When we arrive at a certain income

When we are married

When the baby is born

When we recover from our illness

When our bills are all paid

When we own a new car

When we move into a new home

When some disagreeable task is finished

When we are free from some encumbrance.

Doubtless we shall be somewhat happier WHEN—but not as much happier as we think. Life has a way of presenting new complications, and conjuring up new wants, as fast as old ones are satisfied.

The second delusion is that we can buy a ticket, or pay admission, to happiness.

We seem never to learn that wherever we go we take our happiness or unhappiness with us; and that whatever we do, it is how much of *ourselves* we put into the doing which influences our happiness—far more than what the outside world contributes. The only way we can insure our happiness in these troubled times is to train ourselves to be happy *in spite of*, rather than *because of*, what life does to us. When we succeed in doing this we become adult.

✓   ✓   ✓

It is these two delusions which keep us looking *ahead* or *abroad* for happiness, instead of enjoying the small pleasures right around us—*here* and *now*.

My friend Timothy Crowley used to quote a saying taught him in childhood by his mother: "Ye may go forth in search of happiness, but to find it ye must return."

One of the most important discoveries I have made since this book was first published is that what started as a "hobby" to be practiced on the side, as it were, has gradually grown into a deeply satisfying way of life as well.

As long as I looked upon giving myself away *merely* as a hobby, I was not getting the most out of living. But as giving-away became a habit as well as a hobby, something happened inside of me. I felt a new sense of human warmth in all my relations with people. Friends and business associates seemed closer to me; neighbors and acquaintances became firm friends; and my first contacts with strangers were often delightful adventures which led to, new friendships.

It is never too late, nor is anyone ever too old, to take up giving-away as a hobby. You are probably doing, already, a great many of the things mentioned in this book, and perhaps many others that have not occurred to me. To live a more thrilling life, rich in satisfactions and full of little adventures, you simply begin to look for *still more* opportunities to give yourself, to *still more* people, in *still more* ways, both usual and unusual. At least that is my experience.

Whenever the world grows a bit dull, or I feel low in spirit, I know at once what the trouble is: *I have stopped trying to give myself away.* Instinctively, I look around for some opportunity to share a bit of myself. It seldom takes long to find one. Then I begin to feel alive—to glow with a current of happiness.

✓ ✓ ✓

As I write this, I clearly realize for the first time that this is what happiness really is—*a current.* It is as though each of us were an electric bulb, some of low wattage, some high, but all of us free to draw a supply of happiness from the world's inexhaustible current. And all of us potential disseminators of light and warmth.

No one has ever learned the secret of continuous happiness. Perhaps we could not stand it. Possibly we should burn out, like a spent light bulb. But I am sure every one of us could absorb much more happiness than we do enjoy—without the least danger of burning out!

One thing is certain: When we set out to give ourselves fully and freely, our hearts make direct connection with that great central source of light and power, God, the giver of all good things.

✓ ✓ ✓

"Suppose," a friend asked whimsically, "all of us should suddenly take up your hobby and start 'giving ourselves away' in the fashion you suggest. Wouldn't we begin to bump into each other?"

I have asked myself that same question—seriously. And I have come to a definite conclusion: We would suddenly find ourselves living in the most gracious age in the history of the world, with our lives full of delightful little adventures, our days happy and all too short, and the very air we breathe charged with friendliness and good nature!

Wouldn't you like to live in such an age?

Wouldn't the tolerance and understanding and good will that would be generated by such a spirit give you confidence that in spite of man's stupidity, peace and sanity can be restored to the world?

Isn't this something you and I can do, starting today, toward lifting the blanket of gloom and suspicion that has settled over mankind, while at the same time we earn greater happiness for ourselves?

↗   ↗   ↗

Let the mission of this final chapter, Gentle Reader, be to repeat the invitation extended to you in the introduction: to join me in the happy hobby of giving yourself away, that you and I may do our modest share toward making this troubled world more human, more kindly, more empathetic. In short, *more livable*—for all of us! Starting right away!

THE BEGINNING